Psychology for Pastoral Contexts

A Handbook

Jessica Rose

CANTERBURY
PRESS

Norwich

© Jessica Rose 2013

Published in 2013 by SCM Press
Editorial office
3rd Floor
Invicta House
108-114 Golden Lane,
London EC1Y 0TG

SCM Press is an imprint of Hymns Ancient & Modern Ltd
(a registered charity)
13A Hellesdon Park Road
Norwich NR6 5DR, UK

www.scmpress.co.uk

British Library Cataloguing in Publication data

A catalogue record for this book is available
from the British Library

978-0-334-04552-6

Typeset by Manila Typesetting Company
Printed and bound by
CPI Group (UK) Ltd, Croydon

Psychology for Pastoral Contexts

Contents

Acknowledgements   *vii*

Part 1: The Pastoral Context   1
  1 Pastoral Activity as Participation   3

Part 2: Some Building Blocks in Psychology   13
  2 Mind, Body and Spirit: The Human Being as a
    Holistic Entity   15
  3 Nurture, Attachment and Love (1): Attachment as a
    Natural Impulse   37
  4 Nurture, Attachment and Love (2): Some Pastoral
    Implications of Attachment Theory   47
  5 Sexuality (1): The 'S' Word: What is Sexuality and
    How do We Talk about It?   61
  6 Sexuality (2): Some Darker Aspects of Sexuality   81
  7 Loss (1): 'The Art of Losing'   104
  8 Loss (2): When Grief is Overwhelming   119

Part 3: Some Specific Issues in Mental Health   133
  9 What is Mental Health?   135
 10 Depression   145
 11 Addiction   164
 12 Eating Disorder   179
 13 Schizophrenia and Other Psychotic Disorders   193

Part 4: Betrayal and Forgiveness   205
 14 Betrayal and Forgiveness   207

CONTENTS

Appendix: Reflecting on Your Pastoral Practice   223
Further Reading   228
Index of Authors Cited   234
Index of Subjects and Biblical Names   236

Acknowledgements

I would like to thank all those who have been part of the journey that has resulted in this book, especially Fr John Baggley, Chris Beebee, Hilary Caldicott, Revd Angela Forbes, Charles Hampton, Fr Billy Hewitt SJ, Ian Huish, Patrick Parry Okeden, Revd Michael Paterson, Wendy Robinson, Revd Tom Stevens and Rachel Verney. Particular thanks are due to my husband, Alfred Osborne, for his encouragement, support and wisdom.

The experiences of many people have gone into the making of this book. Names and contexts have been changed to preserve confidentiality.

PART I

The Pastoral Context

I

Pastoral Activity as Participation

What is a 'pastoral context'?

The word 'pastoral' takes us to images with a long tradition in the churches, but which many people find difficult today: images of pastors as shepherds caring for their 'sheep', the people. In the contemporary church we are far less inclined to think of pastors and the people in this way.

We can, however, trace this image to Christ saying to Peter, 'Tend my sheep' (John 21.16). He says this after the resurrection, shortly before he is to leave the disciples and return to the Father. Three times he asks Peter, 'Do you love me?' and three times Peter insists that he does. Each time, Christ responds telling him, 'Feed my lambs', 'Tend my sheep', 'Feed my sheep'. At the heart of a pastoral context is the logic of this encounter: loving Christ is not just a two person relationship – it involves caring for those he loves as well. A pastoral context, then, is one in which concern and practical action for others – and each other – is rooted in a common love of Christ.

'Pastoral' care also has its secular contexts, particularly in education, where it addresses people's needs at one remove from the primary purpose of the organization: the listening, supporting, encouraging or befriending that enables people to make use of what the institution has to offer. Similarly in the context of church life, pastoral care is summed up by Alastair Campbell as 'that aspect of the Church's ministry concerned with the well-being of individuals and communities'.[1] For the purposes of this book, the word 'church' is not used to refer to any particular one

---

1 Alastair Campbell, 1987, *A Dictionary of Pastoral Care*, London: SPCK.

of the Christian Churches but to discuss aspects of community life that tend to be common to them all.

'Man does not live by bread alone' (Luke 4.4). All the same, from the earliest days of church life as described in Acts, it is clear that as soon as communities are formed human needs emerge and require attention alongside teaching and preaching. There are widows who must be provided with food (Acts 6), ill people needing to be healed (Acts 8.7), matters of church discipline to be settled (Acts 15), and 'care of the afflicted' as carried out by a widow thought suitable for inclusion in the church's financial structure (1 Tim 5.3–16).

How has pastoral activity developed?

There is a sense in which pastoral activity as we understand it today is something that can happen anywhere, anytime. Although it is particularly a function of ordained ministry and teams of people are appointed to see that it takes place, essentially it arises from community where a common life of worship spills over into the practical expression of the love of God. It may be an encounter that lasts five minutes as you invite a stranger to join in coffee at the end of a service, or it may be a relationship over several years as you support someone through a long-term mental or physical illness. Life throws up different needs at different times, and in a pastoral context roles are not necessarily fixed. One week you may find yourself listening to my sadness over a lost job or a dying friend, while the next I might look after your children so that you can have a few hours to yourself.

This is the 'Early Church' model: 'Encourage one another and build each other up, as indeed you are doing' (1 Thess. 5.11). The Greek word here translated as 'encourage' is *parakaleite*, from the same root as *Parakletos*, the Comforter who will come after Christ returns to the Father. In the mutual encouragement of the community, we can see, perhaps, the Spirit at work.

It was not until the second century that pastoral responsibility began to be seen particularly as the business of bishops and clergy. This was partly as a function of elaborate penitential systems involving confession and repentance, and partly in relation to the need to understand the place of families in the Church: since the Second Coming had not happened in the first generation it was no longer considered irrelevant to marry and have children.

One of the bishops to pay particular attention to pastoral problems was John Chrysostom (c. 349–407). His sermons on wealth and poverty and on marriage and family life (he was one of the last of the Church Fathers to write about marriage!) are some of the earliest pastoral texts we have.[2] The sixth century gives us 'The Pastoral Rule' of Gregory the Great, the 'pastoral pope' – a treatise for bishops on the care and cure of souls which draws on the lives of the apostles and various Old Testament characters.[3]

In the earlier centuries, however, the pastoral emphasis was sacramental: confession and absolution, anointing the sick, using offerings at the Eucharist to help the poor. At a later stage, the Dominican and Franciscan orders gave new prominence to preaching, and the Jesuits to education and spiritual direction.

By the seventeenth century, we have George Herbert's 'Country Parson' who is all things to all men, at least on a domestic level. His resources are Scripture and prayer through which he is able to embrace the cross, but it is also right for him to socialize and be humorous since 'nature will not bear everlasting droopings'.[4] He works with what is there: the people's frame of reference, their festivals and customs. It is a benevolent patriarchy which with the Industrial Revolution begins to include social reform, led by people such as William Wilberforce (1759–1833) and Charles Kingsley (1819–75), author of *The Water Babies* and a canon of Chester Cathedral.

A further revolution took place in the early twentieth century with the rise of psychoanalysis and other schools of psychotherapy, through which pastoral work developed a psychological frame of reference. Leslie Weatherhead (1893–1976), a Wesleyan minister, was one of the first pastors in this country to take Freud seriously. He acknowledged that Christianity *as it is lived* is open to the charge

---

2 John Chrysostom's sermons, *On Marriage and Family Life* and *On Wealth and Poverty*, are published in translation by SVS Press, Crestwood, New York.

3 For a detailed critique of this history see T. C. Oden, 1984, *Care of Souls in the Classic Tradition*, Minneapolis: Fortress Press.

4 George Herbert, 1981 *The Country Parson*, Classics of Western Spirituality, Mahwah, NJ: Paulist Press, Ch. 27.

of infantile neurosis: a flight from reality (God will comfort me); a false sense of physical security (when in fact Christ promised persecution and death); misusing the cross as an escape from guilt (we are 'let off' because Jesus died in our stead); and narcissistic holiness ('designer' spirituality). Like Freud, Weatherhead saw repressed sexuality as the basis of anxiety. In 1936, he began work at the City Temple seeking out colleagues with a real Christian experience of their own, a psychological qualification and a medical degree. For those who sought their help, a series of six or eight interviews was combined with intercession for healing and simple talks and explanations about psychological processes. The pastoral counselling movement was born.

As pastoral counselling developed, many church pastors learned to speak the language of psychology and use its techniques, albeit applied in a theological context. The pastoral counselling movement also brought a new emphasis on lay intervention, using specially trained members of communities to spread the load. Alongside the pastoral counselling movement, theologians such as Harry Williams, Thomas Merton and Henri Nouwen helped people to think about their faith with personal honesty and psychological intelligence.

As Alastair Campbell also notes, although pastoral activity may include pastoral counselling, it is actually a much broader field. There are also specific differences between pastoral counselling and pastoral activity in general. Whereas a counsellor generally holds back on his or her own views and opinions, the pastor – lay or ordained – can be assumed to represent the shared faith and world view of the community: if this is what we believe, then this is how we might deal with this situation. Unlike a counsellor, the pastor also has access to – and direct responsibilities towards – the whole range of relationships in a community. He or she is also a witness who carries certain expectations: we can draw strength from the role of the pastor as well as from what he or she does or says. Being there and going on being there – as individual and community – is an important factor in the pastoral role of the Church.

For example, a hospital chaplain remarked that not many people ask for her as chaplain, but they do welcome someone to talk to. The fact that she is dressed in a clerical collar is witnesses to the reason why she is there. On a broader level the liturgical cycle whereby the Church celebrates incarnation, death, resurrection and ascension feeds in at a very basic level to shaping the year for the wider community.

As the twentieth century progressed through two world wars, its latter part saw a crisis of identity in many institutions and professions beyond the borders of the Church. Previous notions of hierarchy, authority and gender relations were questioned if not broken down. In *Love's Endeavour, Love's Expense*, W. H. Vanstone charts the changes that took place in the Church from the 1930s to the1960s:[5] a change from being a benevolent parent at the heart of society to being a fringe member of society, from being needed to being needy, from being a Church that has the answers to being a kenotic Church. Similarly, in *The Stature of Waiting*, he points out the progression in the Gospels from activity to passivity, from action to passion, culminating in the moment when Jesus is handed over to the authorities.[6]

In recent times, alongside increasing attention being paid to the training of pastoral workers in the rudiments of psychology and listening skills, we have also seen a return to an understanding of pastoral work that is participatory. Rather than the pastor being the shepherd of the flock, care for each other arises from the love of God experienced in shared worship. It can happen anywhere, anytime, 'to or for, by, with, or from everybody' as Michael Flanders described the London omnibus.[7] Of course, much of the activity involved in fostering the well-being of individuals or communities requires a more structured approach. It may be important that a person can rely on regular visiting or practical help or that a youth group brings people together each week and sometimes that skilled pastoral counselling is available.

---

5 W. H. Vanstone, 1977, *Love's Endeavour, Love's Expense*, London: Darton, Longman and Todd.

6 W. H. Vanstone, 1982/1987, *The Stature of Waiting*, London: Darton, Longman and Todd.

7 M. Flanders, 1957, from his introduction to the song, 'A Transport of Delight', in the revue with Donald Swann, *At the Drop of a Hat*: '"Omnibus", my friend Mr Swann informs me, comes from the Latin, *omnibus*, meaning "to or for, by, with, or from everybody" – which is a very good description! This song is about a bus . . .'

Pastoral activity, then, includes visiting people who are ill, lonely, bereaved or in prison or hospital; conducting rites of passage such as baptism, marriage, funerals; conducting meetings; being involved in education of children and youth work; helping with personal dilemmas; resolving conflict; teaching and preaching; welcoming strangers. It is potentially endless, and one of the hardest things for people involved in it is to know where its limits properly lie.

Pastoral activity as participation

The model of pastoral activity adopted here is rooted in participation in a community, and we will be encouraging self-reflection as well as discussing difficulties you may meet 'out there'. While pastors have particular responsibilities, they too are nourished by the community. Pastoral intervention is seen both as responsive – incarnating the love of God in response to distress – and as redemptive: entering into the life of community with a message of hope.

If you are already involved in a pastoral context you may well have found that there are parts that come easily and others you would rather avoid if possible. You may be a marvellous listener but hate meetings or dealing with conflict; you may be brilliant at getting youth groups or soup kitchens going but dread visiting people in hospital, or doing funeral follow-ups. Each one of us has to work out where we function best according to context, personal inclination and particular gifts, and remember to seek help with the other bits. As you read this book you will be encouraged to draw on your own resources, and question what difference faith, along with prayer, worship and ritual, makes to your own life and that of your community.

A basic axiom in this approach is that a good pastor is not someone who never makes mistakes, but someone who has the courage to reflect on those mistakes and what can be learned from them.

Thinking, feeling and doing

Another basic assumption is that an effective pastoral intervention involves bringing together three things: thinking, feeling and doing. These do not necessarily all happen at once, and the order in which they enter the equation is dependent on context, and may take time. For example, a young college chaplain went to visit a student about whom he was concerned and found him sitting in a room with the gas fire on – but not lit – and the windows closed. There was already a strong smell of gas. Without thinking he reached into his pocket, took out a pipe and asked, 'Got a light?' The student immediately leapt up and opened a window. Afterwards came the realization of what they both had done, and the beginning of the student's long road into working on his feelings.

The chaplain's 'doing' in this instance was exquisitely timed – if unplanned! But in bringing the three factors together, timing is not always easy. If we give people rational solutions at a time when they are not emotionally ready to hear them, or when the practical groundwork has not been done, the effort will be lost. It may also require different people to provide the different aspects of the intervention.

Grace was a well-loved member of a parish where for some years she had been warden and was in church every Sunday. She was, however, becoming too old and ill to cope in her own home. At first, members of the community rallied round, taking meals, visiting, helping her get to hospital appointments, but as her health deteriorated and her anxiety levels rose, they found themselves overwhelmed. The level of feeling grew ever stronger, the vicar being bombarded with their despair and frustration. Grace's relatives had found a place for her to go which was in easy reach, but she refused to discuss it. When the vicar visited Grace, he did not have any practical tasks and was able on several occasions to listen at length to her dread of losing her independence. He felt torn apart between his sympathy for her and the burdened parishioners. He tried a few times to encourage her to consider a move but with no success.

It was only when Grace had had a chance to voice her feelings and know that they had been heard that she was ready to hear the thinking response. One day when the vicar visited, she told him she had been to see the place, but she was still not sure. It was then that he was able to say to her, 'I think the time has come – and your friends and neighbours will be able to visit and enjoy your company rather than worrying about you.' This time she was able to hear what he had to say.

For most of us, one of the three – thinking, feeling or doing – will come more easily than the others, and it can be helpful to identify which of them we need to work at – and even sometimes enlist people who are good at our weaker functions. You may be very good, for example, at chairing a discussion in such a way that everyone is heard and a reasonable decision is reached, but you may need someone else on hand to see that the decision is actually carried out.

Being informed, keeping the faith

Encountering people in a church context also challenges us to reconcile what our faith tells us with what we experience at a psychological level. Although both frames of reference may be deeply informative about the human condition, they often tend to pull us in opposite directions. People often find themselves torn between the desire to follow what they believe to be God's will and the feeling that this is simply unmanageable. For example, a couple having difficulties in their relationship may find themselves facing the possibility of separation. Faith may tell them marriage is sacred, if only they can pray more they will find a way through together, they must learn to forgive; while a psychological assessment of the relationship suggests that perhaps the damage is such that neither will truly flourish if they stay together. Both these approaches contain truth: the question for the couple – as well as for the pastor involved – is to try to discern how to live authentically with their beliefs and the actuality of their situation. What are they actually capable of?

In a pastoral context, faith has to take the primary place in the sense of underpinning the whole enterprise, but this does not mean we can allow it to operate in ways that are dismissive or ignorant about how human beings actually function. From a psychological point of view we will assume that much of our inner life is driven by our primary relationships, and we are not conscious of how this is happening. Much of what goes on in human emotional life is happening out of sight, and we are passive in relation to it: like the 'passions' with which the early monastics battled in the desert, our forgotten or unnoticed experiences and assumptions can take us over without us being aware of what is actually happening. Increased awareness and consciousness of our unconscious life, though never complete, brings greater freedom.

On the other hand, to allow psychological insight to explain away or belittle faith without struggling to understand it also falls short. There is such a thing as grace, as the unexpected movement of the Spirit in a person's life, and this can be mediated by sacrament, by ritual, or indeed by 'the cup of cold water' (Matt. 10.42) given by one person to another. For the pastoral worker, making an honest and respectful path through the situations he or she meets can be a hard journey in which there are many challenges to beliefs or assumptions. This book aims, within a theological framework, to provide some insight and practical guidelines in relation to problems in mental health for pastoral workers – whether in ordained ministry, pastoral teams or simply as members of a church community.

PART 2

Some Building Blocks in Psychology

2

Mind, Body and Spirit:
The Human Being as a Holistic Entity

Mind: conscious and unconscious

There is a saying from the Desert Fathers, 'The thought that is concealed has great power over us.' In the context of desert spirituality, we can take this as referring to the importance of a spiritual guide in the contemplative life: a disturbing thought that you cannot bring yourself to mention to your spiritual father or mother will become increasingly powerful. Freedom – and progress in the spiritual life – lies in being able to share it. Otherwise it becomes more and more compelling, intruding on prayer and possibly even driving you mad. In psychological terms, this saying still holds good: thoughts and fantasies you dare not confide in anyone else tend to become more and more powerful.

We can, however, take the saying to another level. Suppose the thought – idea, memory, expectation – is concealed not just from others, but from yourself. It resides, we might say, in the unconscious, and from there it drives your mood, your behaviour, your patterns of relationship. There is no way of understanding what is going on unless you can bring it into consciousness.

This can take place at the level of habits of thinking or reacting that inform our everyday responses. Such thought habits are sometimes called 'scripts': frameworks of understanding laid down in early childhood, which you do not even think about until you make a conscious effort to identify them.[1] Examples of scripts

---

1 For more on scripts, see Eric Berne, 1974, *What Do You Say After You Say Hello?*, London: Random House.

might be: 'If something has gone wrong it must be my fault'; 'I am an unhappy person'; 'I never fail', and so on. Whatever your own scripts are, they filter your reactions in any situation. As life goes on they can be modified, rewritten or even abandoned, but the point is to be able to identify them and how they are affecting you in order to be able to judge whether some change is needed.

Concealed thoughts also include forgotten experiences from the past – good and bad – that are built into our way of being and affect our reactions in the present. It is important to remember that our hidden mental processes do not only cause difficulties. Yes, they can have great power over us, but they can also *give* us great power – the power to love, to change things, to engage deeply with science and the arts and with many forms of community life.

When Sigmund Freud (1856–1939) developed his theory of the unconscious, he was trying to put into scientific – and therefore rationally accessible – language what was already known by poets and novelists, so that it would become possible to talk about it explicitly. He saw the human being as a dynamic organism sustained by energies that react in different ways under pressure. By learning to access and adjust the flow of these energies his patients could hope to achieve sufficient stability – homeostasis – to lead a life in which it was possible to love and to work: the two essentials, in Freud's view, of mental health.

Freud was, famously, an atheist, but his ideas about the unconscious have been widened and deepened in ways that are compatible with a religious understanding. The first person to do this – and it was a source of deep conflict between them – was C. G. Jung (1875–1961). He expanded Freud's thinking to include the idea of the personal unconscious as a gateway to the spiritual world and also linked to the collective unconscious of humanity in general, rather as the iceberg we see above the waterline is part of a great bed of ice beneath the surface. The unconscious is a gateway to shared human experience, expressed in art and literature, political movements, scientific breakthroughs, religious practice – and in humour. In these deeper regions we find myth, legend and archetype as well as religious symbolism.

Neurological research throughout the last hundred years suggests that there is a physiological basis for understanding the mind in this way. We share with other creatures a 'core' brain that is essential to our survival. These are the structures that evolved way back in our development, and are sometimes referred to as the reptilian brain. From this develops the 'emotional' (or mammalian) brain which governs our need for social interaction and which we share with all mammals. Finally, there is the 'thinking brain' which links sensations with the emotional and survival-oriented areas of the brain. The pre-frontal cortex gives us the capacity to fine tune and even inhibit our emotional reactions – in fact to reflect on our experience and choose how to react.[2]

A child does not come into the world as a *tabula rasa*, but with inherited genetic patterns which we may call archetypes. These are species-universal patterns which are filled out as we grow and develop: our experience 'wires' the brain according to local and cultural styles of living. Language, which is located around the Sylvian fissure, which divides the frontal from the temporal lobe, is a special case of this archetypal inheritance. John Ryan Haule's description of how the acquisition of language relates to brain structure is only one example of how these archetypes influence our development:

The brain constructs its perisylvanian region according to inherited pre-set preferences . . . Later, practice in language builds neural circuits that render our mother tongue easy and resists our learning new languages. The same 'practice factor' can create new neural pathways to restore brain function after injuries. Thus it appears the archetype itself cannot be located in the brain in any absolute once-for-all manner. Its patterning is in some sense prior to the brain it structures. Later, practice wires up neural circuits in accordance with the familial, local and cultural interactions of everyday life. Thus it seems the archetype may not quite be in the brain, rather it uses the brain. Perhaps we have to look deeper, into the genes, to find the archetypes.[3]

---

2 For a detailed description of this, see Sue Gerhardt, 2004, *Why Love Matters*, London: Routledge, Ch. 2.

3 John Ryan Haule, 2011, *Jung in the 21st Century*, Vol. 1, *Evolution and Archetype*, London: Routledge, p. 21.

The relationship between conscious and unconscious

The world we live in is both what we can see, touch, smell, taste and hear, and also unseen, intangible. As we say in the Creed, 'We believe in one God . . . maker of heaven and earth, of all that is, seen and unseen'.[4] Human lives are lived at the intersection of these two aspects of creation. We are part of the physical, cultural world, but we also have some access to the unseen world that lies behind that. Any one of us has an inner as well as an outer world and, just as we connect with each other and with God in our outer, everyday lives, so also we connect with others and with God through our inner processes.

The conscious mind faces outwards and inwards, processing, reasoning, acting in the perceptible as well as in the unseen world in ways that we have access to and can articulate. What psychologists call the unconscious is hidden from ordinary awareness, though it can come into consciousness in many different ways: through relationships, art and literature, prayer, reflection, deep concentration, dreams, therapy – or events that trigger something unexpected. Whenever we – or something that presents itself to us – still the busy-ness of the conscious mind (in prayer, meditation, sleep, deep concentration, falling in love and so on), our consciousness is enlarged and moves on to another level. Our connection with other human beings and with God is potentially deepened.

At an individual level there are all kinds of assumptions about the world we live in that lie behind our normal everyday thoughts and feelings, assumptions that we do not even realize are there until something forces us to challenge them. Together they form what Robin Skynner and John Cleese refer to as our 'mental map': a fundamental understanding of how life works and our place within it which is built up unconsciously through experience.[5] The map itself is constantly being redrawn without our being aware of it.

---

4 *Common Worship*, Order for the Celebration of Holy Communion, Order One, London: The Archbishops' Council, p. 173.

5 R. Skynner and J. Cleese, 1983, *Families and How to Survive Them*, London: Methuen, Ch. 4. This is an accessible and useful book which explains psychoanalytic theory by means of a relaxed conversation between Skynner (a group analyst) and Cleese (the comic actor). The twenty-first-century reader will need to make allowances for gender stereotypes, but the insight gleaned from years in group work and family therapy is valuable and well worth the effort.

For example, Phyllis, a pastoral assistant, was often called upon to accompany people to hospital visits when they were anxious. As a young woman, Phyllis had worked in a hospital as a nursing aide, and she rather enjoyed going with people to their appointments, providing support and helping them communicate with medical staff. Her experience stood her in good stead when her husband was diagnosed with terminal cancer, and she was able to be calm and supportive of him during his many outpatient appointments in the few months that remained to them. Then, not long after he died, she was asked if she would go with an anxious parishioner to an appointment for a scan. She readily agreed – it was, after all, part of picking up the threads of her life now her husband had died – but only a few minutes after arriving at the hospital, she found herself on the verge of a panic attack. The part of Phyllis's 'mental map' in which hospital was a benevolent and rather interesting place where people were helped to get better, had changed into something frightening associated with the death of her husband. It was only when she found herself once more in a hospital that she realized this and that she no longer wanted to do this particular pastoral task.

Much of the 'mental map', of course, is laid down before we can even speak or articulate it. It is formed by experience as infants and children, beginning with our parents, primary care givers and siblings and later including teachers, school mates and other family members. By a process of what is called 'introjection', we internalize other people's attitudes so that they become part of us.

Memory, emotion and making the unconscious conscious

Within the unconscious also are countless memories – good and bad – which we have simply forgotten in conscious life.

Some of these memories have been repressed – blanked out – because they are too painful or frightening to allow into conscious memory. They may reappear in the form of irrational fear or anxiety, panic attacks, dreams and so on. It is not unusual for them to surface during retreats, when all distraction is at a minimum.

Repressed memory can be an important factor in mental ill-health and we shall return to it in greater detail. It is helpful, however, to note that again there is a physiological basis for understanding how repressed memory affects us. In order to survive we – and other animals – need to be able to evaluate situations as they arise. Whether or not a particular situation is dangerous varies from species to species, and we know that animals – human and otherwise – are born with inherited patterns of evaluation. These methods of evaluation are what we call the emotions. When we experience a particular emotion, part of the brain sends messages through the bloodstream and neural pathways to the rest of the body – the whole system is changed by whatever has caused that emotion, focusing attention and preparing to survive a crisis.

These inborn emotions and the patterns associated with them can also become attached to new stimuli as a result of experience. A notorious experiment was carried out by John B. Watson and Rosalie Rayner in 1920 with a child known as 'Little Albert', who initially showed no fear in the presence of a white rat. Watson and Rayner made a loud, sudden noise every time the white rat appeared, and Little Albert became fearful of the white rat, even when the noise was no longer made. The response even became generalized to his mother's white fur coat. Similarly in animals, there can be learned triggers for an alarm reaction – perhaps a place where a mate has been killed, or where a predator attacked in the past.

Emotional reactions are triggered by areas of the brain that are at the interface between those parts of the brain that are older in evolutionary terms (the reptilian brain concerned with basic survival, and mammalian emotional brain) and the human neocortex. A part of the brain called the amygdala is particularly interesting in that it is involved in producing the feeling of fear. In any situation, the amygdala is scanning memory and patterns in the unconscious to determine whether the body's resources should be mobilized. If the stimulus is perceived as threatening, the amygdala 'sounds the alarm' and we may experience an unexplained panic attack or instinctive dislike.

As human beings we have the ability to respond to such reactions by thinking about them as well as experiencing them. The automatic reaction triggered by brain mechanisms may still happen, but we are also able to reflect and ask ourselves whether the current situation warrants the response that is being triggered, rather than simply running away or hitting out. So for example, a child who has been bullied in school may freeze at the very mention of the word 'school'. By helping the child to identify the feelings and what triggers them and also to make a positive effort to relax in the presence of the word, it may be possible to 'undo' the fight–flight response. A delay has been put on the 'amygdala switch' so that the mechanism that triggers it is available to conscious reasoning as to whether the reaction is still relevant.

This is why being able to engage in personal reflection on your situation and your reactions to it is vitally important. It moves beyond 'gut reactions' to an attempt to assess the reality of the people among whom you live and work and provides clues to where your own past experience may be driving your behaviour in ways that are not appropriate to the present.

For example, Simon was a devoted and well-loved minister. His only problem was that he did not know how to say no to any of the demands that were made on him, and in his early forties he suffered a major burn-out. As he reflected on what had brought him to this place, he got in touch with the fact that his mother had become seriously ill when he was five, and died when he was nine. As often happened at the time when he was growing up, little attempt was made to explain the illness to Simon or talk with him about what was going on for him during those four years – which had in fact been a desperate attempt on his part to care for her, so that she would get well. Her death in spite of all his efforts left him with a heavy legacy of guilt.

As a minister, Simon was a very effective and compassionate pastor, but his inability to say no stemmed from this childhood experience where to care for his mother had been a matter of life and death for him. Having identified this and taken time out to care for himself and recover from his exhaustion, he was able to return to work on a more realistic basis that included self-care as well as care for others.

Between you and me – transferring feelings from one person to another

One way in which the past interferes with our functioning in the present is that feelings we do not remember having as small children emerge in relation to people we meet as adults. It is one thing to be consciously reminded of someone from the past by the way a person speaks, acts or whatever; and quite another to find we have strong feelings about a person – or they about us – which seem to come out of the blue. What may be happening is that a feeling from childhood which could not be processed or dealt with then is triggered by the current situation, and may be hard to deal with in the present unless we understand where it is coming from.

For example, you come across someone in your church or your workplace to whom you take an instant and unaccountable dislike. Other people seem to find this person inoffensive but every time they open their mouth, or even walk into the room, you feel irritated, put upon, even undermined. If this is happening, the odds are that this person has a resemblance you are not even aware of to someone significant in your past with whom you had a difficult relationship. While that memory remains unconscious it is very hard for you to do anything about the way you feel. If you can identify it, however, and how it is affecting you, you then have a choice. You might say to yourself, 'Ah, that's why that person is so awful. She speaks just like Miss X who was so horrible to me at school', and you can then continue to dislike her. Or, of course, you can say, 'There is a strange resemblance between the way she speaks and the way that teacher did. But she is an entirely different person in a different context. With this person I have to take extra care to see her as she is and not as Miss X.'

Although this 'transference' of feelings is a technical term in psychotherapy and some therapists work with it directly, it is also something that is going on between people all the time. It means transferring feelings from a past relationship into a present one, without being aware that you are doing it. Again, there is nothing unusual about this, but it is useful to be aware of it as people in roles, such as clergy, tend to trigger it particularly strongly in others.

In order to think about transference, it is useful to distinguish between the content of an interaction and the process that underlies it. The content is the subject matter – a problem to be solved, the state of the church tower or whatever. The process refers to what is going on between two people while the content is being discussed. In *Watching the English*, Kate Fox describes the way English people talk about the weather and points out that people use these conversations to gauge how far each of them is prepared to go in getting closer to each other. At the level of content the weather is pretty boring: we know it is raining, sunny, cold, hot, without needing someone else to remark on it. Yet what Fox calls 'weather-speak' is in fact a kind of code that can be used as a simple greeting, an ice-breaker leading to conversation or a filler or displacement subject to cover an awkward gap. Initial greetings such as 'Nice day isn't it?' are phrased as questions, requiring a response, however trite. They establish a connection, and their point is not the content, but reciprocity. The person who responds, 'Mmm, yes, isn't it?' has agreed to exchange greetings with the other person, and failure to do this can be a serious breach of etiquette. However, you might go further and make a statement of your own, signalling that you are willing to go beyond simply greeting each other. For example, 'Yes, but they say it is going to rain later' might elicit a response such as 'Never lasts, does it?' opening up the possibility of a bonding joint complaint:

> It doesn't really matter: the point is to communicate, to agree, to have something in common; and shared moaning is just as effective in promoting sociable interaction and social bonding as shared optimism, shared speculation or shared stoicism.[6]

This social bonding is the *process* underlying your conversation with the newsagent or your neighbour. Some of it is easily accessible. You may be well aware that you are flirting, or keeping your distance, or hoping to make an impression. These things, however, are only the tip of the iceberg. Most of the process is unconscious, and an important aspect of it is what is known as 'transference'.

How it works is that a person has had a powerful experience in early life that is not in conscious awareness. In adult life those feelings are triggered by other people who in some way remind you of the original person. Through transference we find ourselves

---

6 Kate Fox, 2004, *Watching the English: the Hidden Rules of English Behaviour*, London: Hodder and Stoughton, p. 32.

recruited – and indeed recruit others – to the inner world. It is the stuff of instant likes, dislikes, falling in love, struggles with authority and so on. Perhaps, for example, a parent or teacher has been unduly harsh with a young child. The fear and anger the child experiences are too difficult to deal with and get pushed down into the unconscious. In adult life, however, that child might have difficulty with anyone perceived as an authority figure. Those buried feelings become transferred to someone who is in authority irrespective of how they actually behave. You could say transference is a particular kind of inbuilt expectation.

Sebastian Moore OSB gives a vivid description of how transference can affect relationships between people and prevents us from facing the inner reality:

> By 'transference' I put my guilt, my self-hatred into you. Once you pick this up and start reacting . . . you are backing me up in my flight-from-self . . . (The making of you guilty and wretched *is* my flight-from-self in action . . .) And when you spot what is happening and stop the counter-transference [i.e. unconscious defensive reaction], you cut off the corroboration you have been affording me. I am thrown back on myself and forced to carry on *in there* the business that I have been much more satisfactorily and satisfyingly carrying on *with you*. I founder.[7]

As Moore himself points out, there is no healing in this process in itself. Most of us, most of the time, find another target for those unmanageable feelings.

The way some therapists use transference, however, is to address these strong feelings directly, using an awareness of the process in the session, to explore whether they are being transferred to the therapist. This can reveal feelings that otherwise are hard to name. A reality check may help to discern what actually belongs in the here and now relationship and what seems to be transferred from somewhere else. It may even be possible to provide a different emotional experience which is healing for the client.

---

7 Sebastian Moore, 1977, *The Crucified Jesus is No Stranger*, Mahwah, NJ: Paulist Press, p. 26.

Like many useful tools, understanding the transference can also be a powerful weapon, sometimes used to belittle what are experienced as real feelings. The feelings *are* real, even if they do not really belong in the present situation, and it is vital to respect this. Pastors are not therapists, but it can be helpful to pay some attention to the possibility of transference where your own or another person's feelings do not seem to fit with the situation in hand. Some useful questions are:

- Who does this person remind me of?
- What expectations go with that?
- How like the original person are they really?

Or, if you suspect you are on the receiving end:

- What do I know about this person's previous experience with clergy/women/men/authority figures . . . anything in you, that is, which could act as a 'hook'?
- How is he or she likely to expect me to behave?
- Do I behave like that?

Looking after the 'I'

The 'I' (or ego) acts as a bridge between the conscious and unconscious, which is a risky place to be and it needs protection. There are innate mechanisms for survival built into our brain structure, but as we grow up we also learn how to function in the circumstances in which we find ourselves. As well as a 'mental map' we build in structures and ways of reacting that make our lives manageable. These are what psychologists sometimes call 'defences'. 'Defences' are the means by which material that is too painful, demanding or out of kilter with the mental map is kept at bay in the unconscious. If these defences are threatened, the structure becomes unstable, and the 'I' comes under strain. Some awareness of how they work – your own and other people's – can be useful in understanding what might be going on in tricky situations.

We all have psychological defences, and without them we would be in a bad way. Probably the most important thing to remember about defences is that in themselves they are neither healthy nor unhealthy. Most of the time, we do not even realize they are at work, and it is only where they are causing problems that they need looking at. They are like the walls of your house: they provide the framework of where you live and are essential to healthy functioning. They keep you warm and dry and keep out people you do not want in your house – but if they crumble or become damp, you may not be sufficiently protected. Likewise, if they become too rigid and immovable your house may become more like a prison than a home.

Our defences can also go into overdrive under pressure or cause problems if they continue to function in situations where they are no longer needed. For example, if someone has spent years in a situation where they were treated badly, they may find it hard to react positively to more benevolent circumstances. The defensive habits of the previous situation are carried over and alienate people in the current situation: it can take a very long time to feel safe enough to let those habits go. It is precisely because when they were formed they were essential to survival that they can be difficult to dismantle. If you felt the need to challenge the person in our example because, say, they were being unnecessarily aggressive in meetings, a head-on approach would be unlikely to help. But a gentle exploration of what that person's past experience of meetings has been might open up the possibility of differentiating between the present situation and the past.

For example, Rhiannon spent several years in an abusive relationship. She gradually came to realize that this was not right for her or her partner and managed to separate from him. After a few years, she began a mature and mutual relationship with a new partner and they were planning to marry. All seemed well, except that Rhiannon would become angry and defensive when she was going to spend time with friends or family without her partner. She was aware that he was hurt by this, and one day when she was having coffee with a friend she confided in her. Her friend had herself got married recently and said how strange she found it having a man in the house all the time. She wondered how Rhiannon found that after such a difficult first relationship. Rhiannon realized that the presence of a man – even a gentle and loving man – in her house had triggered a level of anxiety she had not even been aware of, and that she was expecting him to react badly, as her first partner used to, to any suggestion that she might have some life of her own separate from him. She was able to remind herself that this was a different man from her previous partner and her defensiveness was unnecessary. It gradually dissipated.

Again, although we talk about defences as something that we construct, the processes described here take place at an unconscious level. It is not that we sit around working out how to keep ourselves safe: we simply find ourselves acting in particular ways. It is important to remember that there is nothing wrong with defences in themselves, but they can set up patterns that interfere with our lives and relationships.

Here are some of the psychic patterns that are known as defences:

- **Introjection.** From the attitudes and behaviour of our parents is formed what is known as the 'Super-ego' or 'Over-I', which acts as conscience and governs our behaviour. In a benevolent environment, this leads to a positive sense of self, but where a person has grown up in harsh or abusive surroundings these introjected attitudes tell a different story. Sometimes the negative attitudes of parents, teachers, clergy or other authority figures have been so deeply incorporated that it is easier to be hard on oneself than question the original attitudes or the people who held them. An infant or child relies on those very people for survival: it is safer to blame oneself than criticize them. The result is a self-image that is not true to oneself and from that grow guilt, depression, a sense of uselessness or an inability to regulate one's own anger. If you find yourself or someone else ground down by critical voices from within, it is worth asking just whose voices they are and whether they can be challenged.

- **Splitting.** All of us need to compartmentalize life to some extent. One of the most common splits is between the professional and personal self, and this is important to survival. The danger is that we start to think and behave in quite different ways in different situations without even being aware of it. For example, George was terrified of losing his job as a manager, and he became angry with his staff and desperate to placate his customers. He lost track of how he was behaving in different situations, and both staff and customers began to feel they were dealing with two separate people neither of whom was trustworthy. They themselves became split between those who thought George was wonderful and those who wanted him fired.

- **Denial.** A degree of denial – sometimes known as 'mental hygiene' – is vital to mental health: we need to filter out a large portion of the information and experience that comes our way in order to function. (How many people would drive down a motorway, if they spent much time standing on a bridge looking down at what actually goes on there?) It can also be a way of ignoring developing problems, such as, 'I can't really have an alcohol problem, because I never touch spirits.'

- **Intellectualization.** This is another way of distancing yourself, by framing problems in intellectual terms so that it seems you understand them without actually facing up to them. In itself, being able to think as well as feel is a necessary help against being swamped, but it can become dangerous to oneself and others if it is the only mode of operation. (The same also is true of doing everything on a level of feeling to the exclusion of thinking!) Intellectualization is a way of distancing oneself as when doctors take refuge in highly clinical language. It is easier to say, 'There is a carcinoma of the left renal tubules' than 'You have kidney cancer.'

- **Reaction formation.** In reaction formation, the actual emotions are so powerful that they are suppressed, and I experience the opposite to what I really feel. Jim was spending a long weekend walking with his girlfriend, Beatrice, in the Peak District. It was meant as a restorative time after a rocky period in their relationship. During a pub lunch on the Saturday, Beatrice let slip a comment about Jim's best friend that bothered him and kept surfacing in his mind while they were walking that afternoon. That night they stayed, as planned, in an isolated Bed and Breakfast. By the time they had had supper, Jim realized what was bothering him and confronted Beatrice with the possibility that she was considering leaving him for his friend. She admitted that this was the case and that they had been growing closer for some time. For years afterwards, Jim was puzzled by his own reaction then; he felt very warm and protective of Beatrice, even to the extent of letting her have the last piece of toast at breakfast the next day. Only much later did he understand that this was classic reaction formation: he was in fact so angry and afraid of what he might do, that his anger was suppressed and replaced with this excessive solicitousness. If someone seems to be particularly nice to you about something you would expect to upset them, reaction formation may well be at work. The delight I express that you are going for a three-week holiday to the Bahamas may be masking the rage, envy and sense of abandonment underneath. In reaction formation, I am likely to be more than normally helpful – perhaps wanting to help you buy new clothes for the trip, drive you to the airport and so on – rather than to be able to say I will miss you.

- **Displacement.** There is no way of expressing a strong feeling in the proper context so it gets displaced and acted out elsewhere, as in kicking the cat because you cannot shout at the boss.
- **Projection** occurs when some aspect of myself which I am unaware of or unable to acknowledge is projected on to another person This happens on an individual level, but also between families, between communities and between nations. Projection plays such an important part in pastoral relationships that we will discuss it in some detail.

Projection

In Jung's words, 'Projections change the world into the replica of one's unknown face.'[8] Many aspects of ourselves that remain hidden in the unconscious only become visible to us when we see them in other people, giving a distorted picture which may contain grains of truth but is more about the perceiver than the perceived. This psychological mechanism contains the seeds of paranoia, depression and an obscure ability to undermine the other. We do not only project our negative aspects. Idealization can also be a form of projection: unable to access my own positive qualities or capabilities, I see in you what I cannot see in myself.

Table 1: Projection

This schematic representation shows how the unknown (shadow) aspects are seen only when I look at the other person: I do not realize they also belong to me. The conscious 'I' is protected from the unconscious shadow, and the shadow is only seen in the other.

1 Paranoia

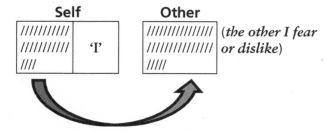

Projecting my own dark side onto the other enables the 'I' to remain confident of my own rightness, while experiencing anger, fear, and a sense of the other as the source of all my problems.

It is perhaps easy to see how this mechanism operates not only between individuals but also between communities (that parish or theological college up the road where they do everything wrong) and nations.

---

8 C. G. Jung, 1959, *Aion: Researches into the Phenomenology of the Self*, 2nd edn, London: Routledge, p. 9.

2 Depression

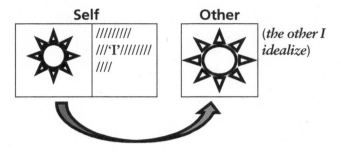

The 'I' idealizes the other, and may experience depression, lack of self-worth and envy because my own positive qualities are inaccessible.

3 Disempowerment

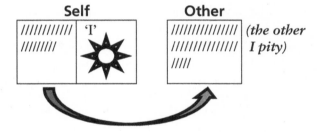

The 'I' experiences cheerfulness, being in control, and the other as despairing and sad.

When projections are identified as belonging to myself and withdrawn from the other, we can both move closer to reality: neither is all good or all bad, but both are able to progress to a more genuine and mutual reality:

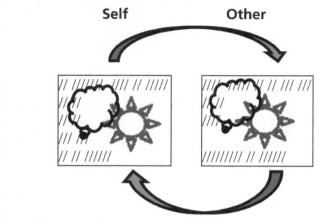

If you find you have a tendency to react strongly to another person, try to explore what it is that you find repellent, attractive, pitiable and so on. See if you can find some of these qualities in yourself (it does not mean they do not exist in the other person as well!).

On the other hand, if you experience a powerful projection from another person, ask yourself if the way you experience yourself with that person is a true reflection of yourself (am I really so nasty, so pathetic, or even so wonderful?). If possible, try a reality check with the other person. This might make it possible to talk about a conflict that is going on, for example, but unless you have permission to do so (for example in a counselling situation) be very careful of making an interpretation. This is only likely to make matters worse between you. Nevertheless, an awareness of what is going on can help you manage the relationship.

For example, Clive, a pastoral visitor, dreaded his times with Mary, a parishioner with severe ME. Mary herself was always cheerful, welcoming and friendly in spite of spending most of her time in a wheelchair. She always greeted Clive with a sympathetic look and by saying, 'Oh, you *do* look tired.' He found himself feeling thoroughly exhausted and came away from these visits drained. In talking it over with a pastoral supervisor, he began to realize that Mary might be projecting her own exhaustion and inability to cope with her situation on to him, and he found courage to begin to address with her how she felt about her illness. Over the next few visits, their relationship became real and energizing rather than unreal and draining.

Remember – projection is not a crime! It is a process that goes on between people all the time and is a key to self-knowledge and the opportunity for change.

The human being as a holistic entity

Although our main focus in this book is psychological, we cannot talk about human beings in terms of mind alone. Everything we discuss here affects us in all aspects of our humanity: mind, body and spirit. An effective pastor – or doctor or psychotherapist – will pay some kind of attention to all three of these aspects whatever the presenting problem. What is important for our purposes about these three aspects is that each of them represents a form of communication, most immediately with other people but ultimately, if indirectly, with God.

They can be presented schematically, as in Table 2 overleaf.

Any of these aspects of ourselves can become ill or function poorly at different times in our lives. They take us into different areas of experience and activity which in turn bring us into relationship with others:

- **The body** is involved in shared physical experience: hugs, fights, sport, eating together, care and nurture, and sex. Its needs form the basis of our economic interdependence at every level – as families, political entities and as the global society.
- **The mind** brings culture into being: myth and story, arts, learning, invention and politics. Together with body and spirit it is responsible for friendship, love and mutuality. Through its psychic processes it is involved with formation of character, and is able to articulate the deep connections between human beings.
- **The spirit** is involved in numinous experience, a sense of awe, and the search for God. Like the body and the mind it

Table 2: Body, mind and spirit

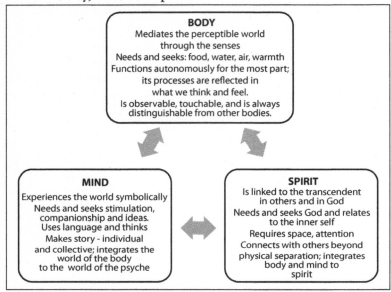

BODY
Mediates the perceptible world
through the senses
Needs and seeks: food, water, air, warmth
Functions autonomously for the most part;
its processes are reflected in
what we think and feel.
Is observable, touchable, and is always
distinguishable from other bodies.

MIND
Experiences the world symbolically
Needs and seeks stimulation,
companionship and ideas.
Uses language and thinks
Makes story - individual
and collective; integrates the
world of the body
to the world of the psyche

SPIRIT
Is linked to the transcendent
in others and in God
Needs and seeks God and relates
to the inner self
Requires space, attention
Connects with others beyond
physical separation; integrates
body and mind to
spirit

is involved in prayer and contemplation, and shares with the mind connections with others that transcend physical presence.

It is not generally easy for us as human beings to be aware of all these aspects of ourselves together and our experience of ourselves and others is often far from holistic. Under pressure body, mind and spirit can become cut off from each other, and one or other aspect may take control or reveal the dis-ease at a level beyond our conscious awareness:

- When the problem becomes one for the body (this is called **somatization**), the problem is expressed in digestive problems, headaches, back pain, addictions, eating disorder, health anxiety, sexual addiction and so on. If we know this as a tendency we can at least learn to listen to what the body might be trying to tell us. James was a Catholic priest who had spent some years as a hospital chaplain and was very good at his job. One day he was invited by his bishop to consider going back into parish work, in particular to a parish with major interpersonal problems. James promised to think about it and was seriously considering the proposal when he realized that ever since he had spoken with the bishop he had suffered a series of migraines and stomach upsets. He concluded this particular move was not for him.

- **Psychologizing** is flight into an attitude that 'it is all in the mind' and can be used to deny the onset of physical disease. It can also take the form of overinterpreting other people as a way of avoiding responsibility for one's own behaviour. Sadly, psychological insight into how nurture, upbringing and environment form our personalities can be transformed into a belief that since other people have made me what I am, then I am no longer accountable.

- **Spiritualizing** is a way of detaching oneself from the realities of body and mind and can be very hard to address in pastoral situations, since it involves a misuse of shared faith resources. It can take the form of extreme asceticism (fasting, sexual abstinence, etc.); dislike and punishment of the body; devaluing of the mind's creativity. Offers to pray can be misused as a way of avoiding working through the problem, as can claims that demonic attack is the cause of all difficulties. We also encounter spiritualizing in phrases like 'Only God understands me.' For example, Sheila was a young woman who had great difficulty in making relationships and suffered badly from depression. Her spiritualized response to this was to long to die, so that she could help God help others.

Being aware of the unconscious in the church community

A primary target for transference and projection is, of course, God himself – the fierce judge, the punishing authority, the abandoning parent, the all-consuming lover. If God is the source of all being, this is no more than we should expect. But the ways God can be perceived are as many and various as human beings themselves. This is one reason for being extremely sensitive in using religious imagery, and being prepared to explore people's own understanding of God and the Christian story without assuming it is the same as your own.

In any church community there will be all kinds of different expectations and perceptions. Belonging to a church in itself challenges our understanding of God, and it can be a devastating experience to find that the God we carry around with us, the God we have personal awareness of, does not match up to the God we find being worshipped in the prayers and hymns of the community, the God we read about in scripture, the God revealed to us in the behaviour of fellow-Christians. Sifting what is illusion in our perception and what is insight into reality is a lifelong process.

Yet, at whatever age we find ourselves within the church community, we have to grow into it; and like any growing experience it can be painful as well as liberating. There are countless people who at one time or another have experienced damage and betrayal within the church. Within the churches we squabble, we split apart, we stab each other in the back, we jostle for power in ways that often surprise and appal non-churchgoing friends and acquaintances. At the same time, membership of any community – a family, an organization, or a church – reflects back to us images of ourselves that challenge our self-understanding. The church itself can become for us a vast family in which we may thrive – or struggle for survival.

The pastor who can build up his or her own self-awareness will be in a better position to help others to do the same, and this is an important step towards building peace in families and in the church community. It gives courage and breeds authenticity. It also confirms that all pastoral involvement inevitably takes the form of participation.

Before looking in detail at specific problems that arise in mental health, we will explore three themes that permeate our mental well-being and dis-ease:

- Nurture, attachment and love,
- Sexuality,
- Loss.

3

Nurture, Attachment and Love (1): Attachment as a Natural Impulse

We are created social beings. In the fourth century, when desert monasticism had become the primary way of living a life of prayer, the monastic founder Basil the Great (d. 378), encouraged people to think that such a life was better lived in community and among people than in desert solitude:

> Man is a tame and social being, not a wild and solitary one. For there is nothing so characteristic of our nature as to associate with one another and to need one another and to need and to love our kind.[1]

To depend upon one another is a good and natural impulse. We are members of one body, 'and all the members of the body, though many, are one body' (1 Cor. 12.12). To nurture one another is also to nurture ourselves.

Our own particular patterns of nurture and relationship are formed very early in life when we are literally dependent on other people for survival. A baby is born with a genetic inheritance that is both personal and shared with other human beings. Those who care for the baby, however conscious their efforts, will also be responding to cues that are built into our brain structure and go way back in the evolutionary scale. Through these interactions with the mother and other caregivers the intense primitive emotions of the baby are contained and regulated, as part of the process of acquiring his or her own ability to adapt to a 'social consensus'.

---

1 Basil the Great, *Extensive Rules* 3, I: PG xxxi, 947.

The neural equipment for this to take place exists in the brain structure. There is 'an inherited set of expectations, recognitions and responses that the baby misses intensely when it fails'.[2] These structures are geared to develop gradually what is known as emotional intelligence – the ability to relate to others and infer what they are feeling. We are not born with emotional intelligence already in place. The part of the brain that is crucial in managing our own emotions and responding to emotional cues is the orbitofrontal cortex: it fine-tunes the intense emotions triggered deeper in the more primitive brain, such as fear, anger and so on. But it does not come ready-made. It develops its neural pathways during infancy – so the kind of attention a baby receives is crucial in this development.

Again, what was intuited by psychologists in the early years of the twentieth century has been confirmed by neurological research in more recent decades. The scientific and therapeutic implications are brought together by Sue Gerhardt, a psychotherapist, who in the 1990s helped found a charity that helps parents to care for their babies:

> I was surprised to discover that we are not born with these capacities . . . it is no good trying to 'discipline' a baby or to expect a baby to control his behaviour since the brain capacity to do so does not yet exist . . . what needs to be written in neon letters lit up against a night sky is that the orbitofrontal cortex, which is so much about being human, develops almost entirely postnatally . . . and doesn't begin to mature until toddlerhood.[3]

Babies, then, rely on adult carers to provide an environment in which they can learn to regulate their emotions. If the adults are overwhelmed by the baby's emotions, it is hard for this development to take place. If our feelings cannot be managed by those around us, it makes it much harder to manage them ourselves. We

---

2 John Ryan Haule, *Jung in the 21st Century*, Vol. 1, London/New York: Routledge, p. 25.

3 Sue Gerhardt, 2004, *Why Love Matters*, London: Routledge, p. 37. This book provides a detailed and accessible discussion of recent research in neuroscience and how early relationships affect the development of the brain.

are not born with a clear idea of 'me' and 'not-me'. In the early months – and even years – you could describe the intense primitive emotions that babies and small children experience as framed by an oscillation between:

- Dependency: I am part of the world and powerless in relation to it, and
- Omnipotence: everything is part of me and everything that happens is because of me.

A good enough experience of caregiving in the early years provides a good foundation for finding a manageable position between those two. This in turn enables us to form attachments that are nurturing for us and also sensitive to the needs of others. This is a negotiation that goes on throughout our lives: it is a lifelong problem to balance our natural tendency to attachment with a sense of insufficiency or need leading to what is called 'anxious' attachment. Sometimes it may seem easier to opt out altogether (a mode of attachment called 'avoidant').

The psychology of attachment

The language of attachment gives us a way into thinking about other-directed love. It has long been accepted by psychologists that nurture is far more than simply caring for the body, and attachment involves far more than getting these physical needs met. A good experience of relationship reflects back a sense of worth and signifies that we ourselves have inner qualities that enable us to develop self-reliance as well as maintain relationships. The search for and tendency to attach ourselves to others is psychologically healthy. If other people were not important to us no one would ever develop the capacity for concern for others that is essential for human relating. How we live this out will be influenced not only by early experience as infants but also by experiences in adolescence when sexuality comes into play.

Two key figures in attachment theory were John Bowlby (1907–90) and Donald Winnicott (1896–1971). Both of them worked with children evacuated from their homes during World War Two. Bowlby also specialized in the psychological welfare of children in hospital. Paradoxically, they found that the children you might expect to be most homesick – those from warm, loving homes – were less homesick than children from disrupted, violent homes.

Among evacuees and hospitalized children, there were three main ways in which they behaved when they were homesick:

- Emotional blackout (moving away from the other). These were children who were not used to being loved and had no expectation of it, so in unfamiliar surroundings they simply retreated into themselves and despaired.
- Total compliance, masking a deep despair. We need to know those around us can tolerate our anger before we dare express it. This is one reason why a parent or carer in the family, who holds things together, often tends to be the target of more anger than a neglectful or abusive parent. These were children who were anxious not to rock the boat. They did everything they were asked, but without really settling down.
- Making a fuss. This was the response of children who had been given enough unconditional love that they believed in their environment sufficiently to try to change it.

Bowlby also analyzed previous studies of infant behaviour and concluded that good caregiving does not come to parents automatically. The infant's own attachment behaviour – smiling, clinging and so on – itself elicits caregiving behaviour. He reached three important conclusions:

- The desire to be loved is an integral part of human life, not simply a babyish or childish need.
- If this desire has not been adequately met during childhood and adolescence we will go on trying to make up that deficiency – but severe failures early on lead to attempts that are either overintense and therefore self-defeating or so well disguised as to be ineffective.

- The main variable in establishing secure attachment is the extent to which parents provide a secure base *and* encourage exploration from that base, i.e. neither ignoring nor smothering the child.

Much work has been done on attachment since Bowlby's time but the patterns he identified have held true, and recent observations of the brain support his analysis.

Being 'good-enough'

The more we are aware, of course, of the importance of early life, the more anxious we may become about parenting. Donald Winnicott, Bowlby's colleague, is famous for his concept of the 'good-enough' mother. She represents an early experience that is not perfect, but which provides enough love and security for the child to develop a strong enough sense of himself to survive painful experiences and even transform them into something positive.

Winnicott himself is an example of someone who creatively transformed his own experience. When he was a small child, his mother suffered from severe depression, to the extent that in later life he wrote a poem where he compared sitting on her lap to lying stretched out on a dead tree. All his life he struggled with depression and fear of breakdown, but he also became a psychoanalyst, and as a writer and broadcaster helped parents, social workers and medical staff to understand how the insights of psychoanalysis could be useful to them.

In regard to the relationship between mother and baby, Winnicott described the importance of leaving enough room for the child to develop a sense of his or her own separate identity as well as providing a secure environment. Too little mothering does not allow the child to build up an internal sense of a reliable presence that will sustain him during absences. Too much mothering, on the other hand, intrudes on the child's self and stifles a natural aggressive tendency, which is actually a potential for development. If this tendency is frustrated, it may turn into violence – or if the child expresses it and the parent cannot survive the aggression, it may become suppressed altogether.

There is no such thing, then, as the perfect parent, because even the 'perfect' parent, who is always there for the child, will stifle that child's development. Some degree of what Winnicott called 'maternal failure' is essential for a child to grow. It is not just all right, but actually important that the mother should sometimes not be there. Timing of course is everything.

We can imagine a small baby who is still physically dependent on the mother, who comes and goes as any mother does. Suppose 'x' is the amount of time the baby can trust the idea of the mother's continued existence when she is not there. If the mother is missing for longer – say 'x' plus 'y' – then the baby becomes distressed, but is easily comforted when the mother comes back. If it is rather a long time, the child may even be angry with the mother, but if she is not unduly upset by that and it is clear that she and her love for the baby survive the child's anger, then the child learns that expressing distress does not lead to annihilation of the mother. However, if the absence is too long – 'x' plus 'y' plus 'z' – this is too much for the baby to handle, leading to potential damage in his or her natural development. Likewise, if the mother is unable to deal with the child's distress when she returns, the child has no chance of learning to manage it for himself.

In ordinary life, of course, there are many separations that are difficult for both mother and baby, and which may lead to her being preoccupied elsewhere (i.e. psychologically absent) just at the time when the baby needs her to be preoccupied with him: illnesses, hospital admissions, financial or other crises, the birth of other siblings. In a secure enough environment, adults who take over the care of the baby or small child can significantly limit the damage – as can taking time to explain to the child, however small, something of what is going on. Small children do not yet have the capacity to work out what belongs to them and what belongs to other people. Events that take place in a young child's life can leave an enormous legacy of guilt if they are not properly explained.

For example, it is a common experience for a new sibling to be born when you are two or three years old. It is a commonplace that this is likely to invoke feelings of resentment or jealousy in the first child, and the way parents contain this is very important.

That is, they acknowledge it and behave in such a way that the first child realizes there is room for him *and* a sibling. If something goes wrong, however, even the best parents may not have the capacity to do this.

Merivan's younger sister was born when she was three. As an adult, she loved her sister deeply, but she was also plagued by depression. When she reflected on her early childhood, she realized that her sister had been in and out of hospital for two or three years as a baby, while a congenital heart defect was treated. The outcome was fine, but what Merivan discovered beneath her own depression was rage that her own childhood had been 'railroaded' by her sister's illness. At a deeper level, she realized that she had resented her sister's arrival and did not know how much her sister's problems were a direct result of that resentment. It was only as an adult that she was able to look back and realize that the things that happened to her sister were nothing to do with anything she felt or wanted at the time: they had simply happened.

Insecure attachment is also at the root of separation anxiety – anxiety or even panic that sets in in the absence of a loved person. Separation anxiety becomes extreme where a person's sense of self is so damaged that he or she can only find themselves in the other. Separation generates massive anxiety, because the very sense of self is threatened by the disappearance of the other, just as a baby's survival is threatened by the too long absence of the primary caregivers.

Who is caring for whom?

Winnicott was able to transform his desire to care for his mother into a lifetime's work of not only helping others but also feeding an immense amount of understanding about the importance of early relationships into society itself. Deprivation is a mysterious thing. Its legacy can be to leave us distant and cold hearted or it can give us a wealth of compassion for others. Part of such compassion is based on a real understanding of what it is not to have one's needs met; but it can also arise from projecting one's unmet needs on to others. There are, alas, many caring people who cannot care for themselves, like Simon in the previous chapter.

Much good care takes place on this basis but sooner or later there will be a reckoning – either in the form of burnout or what is known as 'compulsive' caregiving which becomes intrusive, and serves the need of the carer more than for those being cared for. In a needy community such compulsive caregiving – and the needs of the person doing it – easily go unchallenged, and it is a skilled pastor who can harness its power for the benefit of both carer and cared for.

Toolkit: some useful things to remember about attachment theory

Attachment behaviour is any behaviour that involves getting closer to another person – which may be welcome or unwelcome to the other. This may be anything from sitting next to a particular person at meetings or sending frequent texts to making sexual advances. Some important things to remember about attachment behaviour are:

- It is not the same as, but is as important as sexual behaviour.
- Our ability to do it is essential to making relationships.
- It is present and active throughout life in some form or another and is not in itself regressive.
- It is activated when a bond is threatened or requires maintenance ('It's ages since we actually did anything together for fun . . .').
- It is recognized and complemented by care-giving behaviour.

Our need for love is healthy, and since attachment is so crucial to our well-being, a degree of anxiety about it is natural. Manageable anxiety allows for:

- Self-reliance: living within one's own space, and being able to move – and allow others to move – in and out of it. A self-reliant person is able to explore inner space, but is also aware of limits to his or her self-sufficiency.

- Other-directed love (attachment) which is able to give and receive support and nourishment.
- Interdependency at a personal and communal level that is able to acknowledge and think about how we are affecting each other in relationships.

Insecure attachment generates various forms of anxiety, especially separation anxiety. The kind of early experiences that generate anxiety around attachment include: being unwanted or experienced as a burden; severe discontinuity in care; threats of desertion or threats to stop loving. Even if these are unintended by parents or caregivers and are the result of events in the family beyond anyone's control they can still be experienced by the child as focused on him or herself. Again, family attitudes that see, for example, love as weakness, anger as sin or grief as childish can have a similar effect.

At any time in life, an event that means our usual attachment behaviour does not produce the needed response, such as bereavement, divorce, illness, preoccupation with work or money worries, can lead to excessive anxiety around attachment which tends to take one of three forms:

- Moving away (avoidant) can lead to a fierce independence that says 'I don't need anyone'; 'Don't intrude on my space, and I won't intrude on yours', as in the Simon and Garfunkel song: 'I am a rock, I am an island. And a rock feels no pain; And an island never cries.' Basically this person has given up on attachment behaviour.
- Moving against (hostile) is often seen on a day-to-day level, when a person who is late home meets a furious 'Where have you been?' response. It can be a sign of a healthy confidence in the relationship, but can also become a generalized attitude that is overcritical and angry.
- Moving towards (dependent) is clinging and demanding. It may also take the form of 'compulsive caregiving', where sadness and anxiety are projected on to other people who find they are being looked after whether they want it or not.

The good news is that although early experience does have a profound influence, a loving, mutual relationship at any point in life can help build the capacity for secure attachment. We will explore this in the following chapter.

4

Nurture, Attachment and Love (2)
Some Pastoral Implications
of Attachment Theory

The various ways in which people become attached to each other are often a source of anxiety in pastoral relationships. As Christians, we are supposed to 'love one another' (John 13.34). We are 'the body of Christ and individually members of it' (1 Cor. 12.27). If one member suffers we all suffer; if one rejoices we all rejoice. Within this interdependence of being, however, the Church is – rightly – wary of attachment between members. It generally teaches a spirituality of non-attachment that is important if communities are to hold together as communities. When this works well, it allows the community and its rituals to carry more than individual relationships can. All too often, however, non-attachment slides into a spirituality of detachment which is something else altogether and does not help people to experience the love of God.

Attachment and power are closely related: a person to whom we are attached becomes powerful for us. Of course, we need to be vigilant about this. Yet, in this chapter we shall also argue that it can contain the seeds of transformation.

Anyone in a pastoral role will find themselves the target of parental and other projections: people will react to you as to significant figures from their own lives. You may find yourself seen as authoritarian, depressed, distant, intrusive, rejecting, able to fix anything that goes wrong – or any number of other things. It is important to be able to remind yourself and others who you are, at least from time to time. This is where your own friends and family are invaluable, restoring you to your own size and shape.

People easily become dependent on good pastors. In particular, where you spend a lot of time listening to someone, perhaps sharing intimate story and feelings, you may find anxiety, regression or dependency entering in. All too often pastoral workers are alarmed by dependency and inclined to cut off altogether. Such a relationship can end in an 'x+y+z' abandonment which means nothing has been made of the experience – so the cycle begins all over again with someone else.

Sometimes, however, adult relationships can pass through similar phases as those in the life of a small child gradually learning self-reliance. With some people – but by no means all – it may be possible to address the anxiety directly, in such a way that the person is able to take responsibility for their feelings and move on.

Some risks in helping relationships
Helping relationships carry particular risks to do with attachment and dependency both for the helper and the person being helped. Being a good helper carries the risk of being seduced into an unmanageable relationship. What might begin as flattering (you are the only one who understands me) can become:

- Frightening: What have I taken on here?
- Exasperating: I have given so much to this, and nothing ever changes.
- Infuriating: This person is taking over my space.

Exasperation can creep up on us very easily. Philip, a parish priest, began to dread Saturday mornings. Each week, he got a call from Amy, the choir director, complaining bitterly about choir members not turning up for the Friday night practice. At first, Philip was sympathetic and tried to work with Amy on persuading people to come to practices, but nothing changed, and after a few months he felt no more sympathy, just exasperation. He was becoming seriously angry, and even listening to Amy's messages, if he did not answer the phone, enraged him. He found himself longing to get rid of Amy and casting around in his mind for someone else who might be able to take over the choir – or even if there was some way of doing without a choir altogether.

When feelings like these arise, it is very important to listen to them. This can be painfully difficult for Christians who feel they should be struggling to love and to give, and should not have negative feelings about the people in their care. Nevertheless, such feelings are important cues as to what is actually going on in the relationship and making time to think about them, and maybe discuss them with a trusted person, enables you to learn from them rather than 'acting out', that is to be driven by your feelings into doing things that you would not do if you were able to think clearly.

For example, Jeremy was a newly retired member of a parish eager to use some of his new-found leisure in helping out. He was asked by the pastoral team to visit Tom, an elderly, disabled man, who lived nearby. Tom was an interesting and engaging person, and Jeremy fell into the habit of calling in on him each day on his way to fetch his grandchildren from school. As time went on, however, Tom's dependence on him became so shot through with anxiety that he was ringing Jeremy up four or five times each morning to make sure he was coming that afternoon. It became very difficult to tell Tom if he was going to be away on holiday, or if he simply needed to do something else that day. Naturally Jeremy became exasperated and sometimes quite angry.

Tom's life was very confined with limited opportunities to widen his horizons, and Jeremy's visits had become so important in his landscape that Jeremy felt trapped and put upon. Some days he just wanted to stop going to see Tom without even telling him. Other days he just felt bad: he was fond of Tom but he could not meet his needs, and he also did not want to fail on his first pastoral assignment.

Both he and Tom were fortunate enough to belong to a well-functioning parish community, where other people were available to share this genuine but unmanageable need. Being new to the pastoral team Jeremy was nervous about talking his problem over with the other members. He felt he had let himself become overinvolved in a way that other team members would disapprove of.

When he did talk it over with the team, it was a relief to discover that the problem was a familiar one, though it was clear he did need help in setting some boundaries. When he looked at Tom's situation with the others he realized that he was not the only person on whom Tom relied. There was some support from Age Concern and from the people in the flat above, and even without Jeremy someone was in touch with Tom most days.

It was agreed that Jeremy would continue to support Tom, but a second pastoral visitor was introduced, so that he could begin to space out his visits. He was also encouraged to use the answerphone to field Tom's calls, and not to ring him back but simply be reliable in visiting at the time he had promised. At first, Jeremy continued to feel he was letting Tom down, but over time Tom accepted the more widespread support, and Jeremy felt able to sustain his friendship with him without feeling trapped.

Pastoral carers also have needs and risk becoming overinvolved with those that they help, often without noticing it is happening. To be part of someone's healing process can be a powerful draw and make it hard to hold on to one's own role. An over-close attachment is something we can easily fall into.

Kathy, a curate in a small parish, began supporting Clare, who was suffering from severe postnatal depression. Clare's husband worked long hours, and she spent much of the week alone with the baby. Being in church simply made her feel guilty about her depression, since she felt she was expected to be joyful about new motherhood: the fact that she was almost suicidal and could not bond with her baby was something she dared not speak about, and she stopped going. Kathy, who had been encouraged by the presence of a family with a small baby in the congregation, got in touch with her, and Clare confided in her about the depression. Kathy was sympathetic and encouraged Clare to speak to her doctor and get professional help, and she also began visiting Clare and the baby each week.

Six weeks later, Clare was feeling stronger and more closely bonded with her baby, but she was still fragile. Just at that time Kathy was called away because her father was ill, and it was a month before she returned to the parish. One of her first thoughts was to get in touch with Clare and arrange to go round, and she left an answerphone message. A day or two later, she received an email from Clare saying that she was fine and did not need to see Kathy any more. Perhaps she would see her around in church someday.

Initially, Kathy felt hurt, and was tempted to accept what Clare had said at face value. She also felt angry and rejected. When she reflected on the situation in prayer, however, she began to suspect that Clare was feeling abandoned and pushing her away, because she was frightened of her own dependency on Kathy. She waited a few days and rang at a time when she thought Clare was bound to be in, and they managed to have a conversation. Kathy affirmed her real concern for Clare and also her regret that she had been called away so suddenly. She asked again if Clare would like to see her, and Clare said that she would. Perhaps, however, she could bring the baby round to see Kathy instead of Kathy visiting her?

The change of venue represented a shift: Clare was no longer the dependent person needing to be visited at home. She acknowledged that she had felt cross and upset, when Kathy suddenly went away. They continued to meet regularly, and Clare continued to recover, though she still depended on Kathy's support. Kathy's next absence was her three-week summer holiday. This time Clare was prepared for her absence, and they scheduled a meeting for Kathy's return. When they met, Clare said that she had missed her, but she had managed various things on her own, and this had increased her confidence. It was not so much that she had managed without Kathy as that she knew Kathy would be coming back, and she could manage on her own in the meantime. Something had shifted inside her so that she felt more self-reliant.

Clare was moving on from the depression. In psychological terms, she had learned that Kathy was a trusted caregiver and was able to find in herself an internal caregiver who was able to draw strength from her experience with Kathy and also care for her baby. Meanwhile Kathy struggled with herself. Of course, she wanted Clare to move on, but she realized she would miss the intimacy of their talks and being special in the lives of Clare and the baby. It was around this time that the question of baptism came up, and it was agreed that Kathy would baptize the baby. In the ritual of baptism, she found healing for herself. It honoured the healing work she and Clare had done together, reminded her of her priestly role and restored Clare and her baby to the wider church community.

Risks in being helped

Being the person who is helped in a relationship carries its own risks, including:

- Anxiety about rejection: how will I cope with this person – or this person with me – now I have told them so much about myself?
- Fear of betrayal: can I trust this person to respect my confidence? What seemed safe and protected inside me now feels exposed.
- Disillusionment: when we talked, this person really seemed to understand and care. But when we are in church, she treats me just like anyone else.
- Fear of becoming dependent: I have always fended for myself. I don't want to have to rely on other people.

Blankets, teddy bears and building inner reliance

Becoming self-reliant is a task that is never complete, and relationships throughout our lives are part of the process. Some relationships are lifelong. Others have a transitional quality: they provide a particular kind of help at the time we need it and become part of our inner world, rather like Clare's relationship with Kathy.

It was Donald Winnicott who introduced the phrase 'transitional object' to refer to something that acquires great significance for a period in our lives – like Linus's blanket – but which becomes unnecessary as we mature. The blanket or teddy bear, which has to be taken with you wherever you go and be there in bed at night, makes a bridge between internal and external reality. It mediates between sleeping and waking: the child cuddles it while going to sleep and finds it on waking up. The teddy bear has its own existence, is constant, and survives the child's love and hatred (being cuddled, thrown about, forgotten and so on). It also leads a life created in the child's mind. The child has rights over it – but is not omnipotent. He or she cannot make the teddy bear something it is not. Eventually, it simply loses its significance. The emotions become diffused over many objects, and in health this leads in turn to cultural richness. But that experience of the teddy bear's survival is not lost.

Survival is also an important part of what parents do for children, what communities do for individuals, what pastoral workers and carers do for the people in their care – and what God does for human beings. We find this over and over again in the psalms. The psalmist rages, complains, despairs – and when all that is out of his system, there is the going-on-being of God (for example, Psalms 4, 10, 12, 13).

Transitional objects also exist between people. They include gifts people give each other, objects 'of sentimental value', such as a dead mother's jewellery or a lucky silver dollar. They help to bridge separations, so that a person who has to be away for a while might give someone they love a book, or a special stone or a ring – anything that represents their presence while they are away. They can mediate a transition from a subjective dependency – about me – to an objective interdependency – about us.

Where a child is insecure and anxious, a transitional object can also become a fetish. One of Winnicott's most famous case studies concerned a seven-year-old boy obsessed with string.[1] He played with it, tied up furniture with it, but he also did disturbing things like putting it around his sister's neck or hanging himself upside down with it.

When this child was three, his mother had twice been taken into hospital and Winnicott identified the string play as wanting to tie the mother to him. After he talked with the boy about how he felt about the separation, the string play stopped, though it still recurred when the mother suffered a major depression (a psychic separation) or had to go into hospital (a physical separation). The

---

1 D. W. Winnicott, 1990, 'String: A Technique of Communication', in *The Maturational Process and the Facilitating Environment*, London: Karnac Books, pp. 153–7.

string was an attempt to communicate, and Winicott's intervention worked, because it took place at a point where the original experience was close enough to consciousness to emerge, and there was still hope for the relationship between mother and son. Even though it returned at times of stress, it was now understood for what it was.

Winnicott's case study reminds us of an issue that runs through many pastoral relationships. There is no such thing as a perfect childhood, though there is certainly such a thing as a good enough one. Where experience has fallen short of the good enough, damage is done. Like the evacuated children who did not know how to protest at their homesickness, people often find it difficult to express their feelings about the damaging effects of their early lives. Again, as Christians, they feel they should be quick to forgive; they are anxious about getting caught up in a 'blame culture' which many people feel is fostered by counsellors and therapists.

As in the story of the string, almost all parents strive to be good parents. No one sets out to neglect or damage their child. In the 'string' story, the mother is loving and caring, but she becomes overwhelmed by both the inner and outer world, and this happens to most people at some time or other. Parents themselves have been children and may or may not have learned from their own parents how to care adequately for a child.

What we find, over and over again, is that pasting over the cracks is not helpful. This does not mean that we have to blame or hate our parents for ever. It does mean that we have to allow ourselves to be angry at ways in which they have behaved: to be too quick to understand can be an obstacle to true understanding. And there are also situations where parents and families are damaging – in the present as in the past – to an extent where a clear separation is necessary for a person to survive. This is rarely an easy matter, and a person going through it will need considerable support to survive the guilt and loss involved.

Between trust and terror: a spirituality of attachment
When it comes to making sense of attachment spiritually as well as psychologically, pastoral workers have the advantage over

counsellors and therapists of being able to talk within the framework of shared belief. This does not mean applying soothing words as a sticking plaster for pain, or piling on guilt with judgmental statements. What it does mean is that if you are prepared to grapple yourself with what faith means to you – its problems and doubts as well as its resources and support – you can work within a context that draws on all that faith has to offer. We can be avoidant, hostile or clinging in relationship to God just as we can with human beings. To be loved is not always easy.

In a poem about her newborn son, Anne Ridler (1912–2001) describes him as a little boat:

> Frail vessel, launched with a shawl for a sail,
> Whose guiding spirit keeps his needle-quivering
> Poise between trust and terror.[2]

Here Ridler names a fundamental aspect of the human condition. To live between trust and terror means living as human beings, who cannot conveniently divide our experience into safe and unsafe but have to accept that these are interrelated. Without risk there is no development. Thus there is no simple straightforward answer to the risks that are present – on either side – when we enter into a pastoral relationship. The fears – of becoming dependent, of being depended on – and indeed, of *not* being depended on – are genuine and important. Many an attachment has been formed in a pastoral context that cannot find an adequate response – either because of the situation the people are in, or because the other person simply does not feel the same way. It requires a 'guiding spirit' to navigate through them.

As we have seen, attachment is a natural and essential impulse. Through it we learn to care and be cared for: to live with enough trust that we are not overcome by terror. When strong attachments are threatened we become vulnerable to separation anxiety, which is itself a form of terror.

---

2 Anne Ridler, 1994, 'Choosing a Name', in *Collected Poems*, Manchester: Carcenet Press, p. 123.

The Danish philosopher Søren Kierkegaard (1813–55) tells us that 'whoever who has learned to be anxious in the right way has learned the ultimate'.[3] Anxiety, though potentially destructive, is also the key to freedom, informing us of choice, self-awareness and personal responsibility. If we are able to use it rather than be overwhelmed by it, it can enable us to move from an unconscious state, which either prevents us from acting or drives us to act out, to the conscious reflection which enables us to choose how to act.

'There is no fear in love, but perfect love casts out fear' (1 John 4.18). It is easy to talk glibly about love as something we can rely on, but loving and being loved are complicated for human beings in a fallen world. A thirteenth-century mystic, Hadjewich, explored the fears that are inherent in love in some detail. Hadjewich was a beguine, a woman who lived a life of poverty and contemplation without taking vows as a nun. Not much is known about her life, but we have her letters and poetry in the tradition of medieval love mysticism. She, of course, describes her journey as a contemplative, but what she has to say about her journey into the love of God also throws light on love between people.

Hadjewich had an early vision of the tree of knowledge of God, growing upwards from faith into love. God lets himself be experienced as love by the person who goes out to meet him with love (the path of trust) but the 'touch of love' throws our minds and senses into commotion (leading to a state of terror). By seeking the being-in-One which is not absorption into the One, we learn what it is that relates us to other human beings. She writes about the 'fears' of love that develop as love grows between the contemplative and the Beloved (Christ):[4]

- I am unworthy.
- I cannot be loved enough.

---

3 Søren Kierkegaard, 1980, *The Concept of Anxiety*, ed. and trans. Reidar Thomte, Princeton, NJ: Princeton University Press, p. 155.

4 Hadjewich, Letter 8, in *Hadjewich: The Complete Works*, The Classics of Western Spirituality, Ramsey, NJ: Paulist Press, 1980, p. 64ff.

By living these fears rather than denying them, she suggests that we can come to maintain a state of what she calls 'noble unfaith'. This is superior to certainty and, she says, 'greatly enlarges consciousness'. It keeps the heart vigilant.

Hadjewich's seven names of love are all resonant with Anne Ridler's 'needle-quivering poise':

- The **chain** binds and grasps, joining her with delight while encircling her so tightly she will die of pain. It is the place where we know each other through and through, especially in the Eucharist. In the ultimate union of the Eucharist we are also shown our separateness: Christ is not consumed and neither are we.
- The **light** shines as both condemnation and enlightenment. It can illuminate us (trust) or expose us (terror).
- The **live coal** is a swift messenger that both inflames and cautions us – as in Isaiah 6.7.
- The **fire** devours without distinction, and Hadjewich contrasts it with
- the **dew** that is appeasement, calm, kiss and sweetness.
- The **living spring** is flowing, growth, hidden ways; it engulfs everything.
- **Hell** – the final name of love – is unrest, torment, 'for there is nothing love does not engulf and damn': 'No grace is there.'

These names sum up all that we can trust and all that we can fear in love: how can this relate to everyday experience of relationships? Somewhere between trust (everything is cared for) and terror (everything is in chaos and undone) lies the realism of mutuality. This always involves living with risk: taking risks with and for each other. So, for example, where distance meets warmth it may come in from the cold. Where anger is acknowledged it may find what it needs in order to let be. Where dependency is accepted without collusion, it may help build self-reliance.

Whatever we are prepared to do in risking dependency and developing trust, we all have to live ultimately with the elusiveness of God – with experience of absence as well as presence. We need, therefore, other human, physical people to remind us of our own reality. For example, when Mary received the announcement from the angel Gabriel that she was to bear the Messiah, she went straight away to her cousin Elizabeth – and it was with her that she was able to take in the inconceivable truth. Her experience was reflected in Elizabeth's joy (Luke 1).

Even where love is reciprocated, however, there is no abiding city. The most loving relationship is eventually separated by death. However rich and dependable the relationships with which we surround ourselves, we also have to learn in the end to live as individuals the life intended for us by God. However much I may love and trust and depend on anyone, the meaning of that relationship is held by something far greater than anything we can do between us. What happens in the here and now is a reflection of the love between the persons of the Trinity and the love of God for us. To take that up consciously is to be transformed.

There are many biblical stories that speak about this, and they will have different significance for different people, but one of the most powerful is that of Mary Magdalene's deep attachment to Jesus. According to the fourth Gospel it is she who first discovers the empty tomb on the first Easter morning (John 20). She fetches Peter and John, and having seen that the tomb is empty they return home. Mary stands weeping by the tomb, unable to leave the place where Jesus last was, even in death. When he appears and she mistakes him for the gardener, she says, 'Sir, if you have carried him away, tell me where you have laid him, and I will take him away' (John 20.15). Then, after she has recognized him, his first words are 'Do not hold on to me', and he sends her out to tell the others that he is ascending to his father (John 20.17). Mary has to move beyond her ordinary, human attachment, to embrace the place of Jesus as the risen Christ, who is not simply given back to his disciples as he was before the crucifixion, but will ascend to 'my God and your God', taking all their humanity – and the wounds of his passion – with him.

Toolkit – how is an understanding of attachment helpful?

- Get in touch with your own attachment strategies. What is your default mode – to move towards, to move away, or to move against? Being aware of this helps to form inner boundaries. If you have trouble saying no, ask yourself what you think will happen if you do. If you have trouble asking for help when you need it, try it out with someone you trust.
- Listen to your own anxiety, frustration, exasperation. Doing this makes it easier to work out how much they belong to you and how much to the other person or situation. From there it may become easier to confront a difficult attachment without being rejecting.
- Develop consistency. So often pastoral workers are drawn into offering more than they can give, or assumptions are made about availability which are simply not realistic. To be firm about what you can and cannot offer is not withholding help – it is giving it consistency and thereby making it effective.
- Confronted with a situation where someone has become overdependent, believe that 'this too will pass'. Avoid getting sucked in, but think of yourself as a transitional object: as such you will eventually lose significance. Being able to sit the situation out, knowing where your own boundaries are, while believing that the process carries meaning for the other person might enable them to move on.
- Believe in people and do not take personal responsibility for their survival. At the same time, if you know you have become important to someone be prepared to take some responsibility for that. Talk it over with a third party. Be willing to acknowledge you may have hurt someone, whether you intended to or not.
- With many demands on you it can sometimes be easy to lose track of who you are. Make space to remind yourself – with family or friends, in prayer, in music or sport. Try to make sure you do not go more than a week without

carving out significant time for whatever restores you to yourself.

- Remember that your community is a resource. Think about ways in which its members can become interdependent rather than depending heavily on you. Face your own need to be needed if this is necessary.
- Reflect on the shared rituals of your church community and what they hold for you and for others.

5

Sexuality (1)
The 'S' Word: What is Sexuality –
and How do We Talk about It?

Sexuality is the second of our three major themes. In this chapter, we will look in general at sexuality and in the next discuss some of its darker aspects. While it is only possible here to highlight some aspects of sexuality, the aim of these chapters is to encourage thinking and reflection.

What is sexuality?

More or less anyone finds sexuality hard to talk about, because it is closely bound up with our own intimate feelings and identity as well as underlying ways in which we are attracted to others. In churches in particular, discussion can be difficult, because there are strong prohibitions around sexual behaviour. The underlying assumption, even if it is not the practice within the community, is that the only truly acceptable face of sexuality is marriage and childbearing.

As the 'legitimate' aspects of sexuality, these tend to become idealized. Yet, it is hard to ignore the fact that even here people run into difficulties, become anxious, suffer and even abuse each other. Often it seems that at one extreme the churches affirm sex as a gift from God while paying scant attention to difficulties and damage, while at the other they identify sex with sin. Sexuality as a subject for discussion comes to mean the 'problem' areas – usually homosexuality with a bit of gender relations or child abuse thrown in.

This is inevitably a distortion, since there is far more to sexuality than this. We are all born into a sexualized world. Sexuality is the basis on which we become members of a family and acquire our genetic inheritance. It pervades our hopes, fears, taboos, achievements and failures and is built into our human nature. It also reflects God's creative power that suffuses the universe.

Sexuality, then, is far more than explicitly sexual behaviour or even gender identity or orientation. It touches us at the most private and vulnerable level, involving how we are accepted and rejected, consciously and unconsciously, in relation to our sense of self. It runs through the formation of who we are and is, of course, deeply involved in the relationships we form. We could say that at this individual level, sexuality has two aspects:

- how I experience and understand myself,
- how I relate to other people and the world around me.

These are lifelong questions, which grow and develop as we ourselves do. They are also spiritual questions and exist in the tension between being fully human and embodied and being also in the image of God, drawn to that which tells us our true name.

Nowhere else do body, mind and spirit touch each other so closely and nowhere are we more inclined to try and split these three apart – to escape into sexual acting out, mind games or a spirituality divorced from our full human being. Because it is so hard, even now, to talk honestly about our sexual desires and feelings, they tend to get driven underground and emerge where we least expect them. So we find, for example, the charismatic celibate priest who leaves in his wake a string of damaged women or even children; the fierce opponent of abortion who secretly has one herself to protect her reputation; the ascetic who cannot control the urge to masturbate; the man who rushes into marriage and fatherhood, because he is terrified of his sexual longing for other men.

It is because sexuality is so powerful that we do our best to package it, manage it and set limits around it. These limits are, of course, essential if we are to live out our sexuality without damage to ourselves and others. On the other hand, sexuality does not tolerate being ignored and is at its most dangerous when we try to pretend we are someone or something we are not.

Whether a person is male or female, single, married or celibate, gay or straight, with or without children, is no predictor of how fulfilled they feel as a person. Whatever our situation, we still have to tangle with that most difficult of people – myself. In Elisabeth Taylor's short novel, *Hester Lilly*, Hester, a lonely and sad young woman, meets an old lady, Miss Despenser, who mocks her for being frightened of adders:

> When she had finished laughing, Miss Despenser said: 'When I go into the town to get the cat's meat . . . I see myself walking towards me – in a long panel mirror at the side of the shop. "Horrid old character," I used to think. "I must change my shopping morning." So I changed to Fridays, but there she was on Fridays just the same. "I can't seem to avoid her," I told myself. And no one can.'[1]

Sexuality and the life cycle

Different sexual energies come into play with growing up, negotiating family life and leaving home, with romantic love, physical longing, forming – or not – a permanent relationship, becoming – or not – a father or mother, ageing, making way for a new generation.

At the heart of the Christian faith is a God who became an embodied human being like us. We do not believe that Jesus ever had a full sexual relationship with anyone, but we do know that he was very much alive as a physical human being. As a child, he was fed from his mother's breast, and he grew up as the son of a carpenter, learning his father's trade. He drew people to him, and he could be tender, intimate, angry, joyful or exhausted; he related easily to women as equals in an age when this was unusual. He was profoundly aware of who he was.

---

1 Elisabeth Taylor, 1954, *Hester Lilly*, reprinted 1990, London: Virago, p. 36.

Each one of us is also an embodied human being, born with untold potential. As we grow up we pick up all sorts of messages about who we are and where we fit in from parents, siblings, schools, significant others with whom we identify – or from whom we try our best to be different – as well as from the relationships we witness and the hopes and desires we experience for ourselves.

We have already discussed the importance of nurture in the early years of life. Infancy is also when we learn for the first time about love and tenderness as well as about shame and responsibility and what is and is not acceptable. How our parents and first caregivers first touched and held us is remembered by our bodies – and indeed by the neural pathways in our brains. We also become aware of ourselves as gendered human beings and how we are the same as or different from other males and females including our parents.

All this is part of separating out from our parents and becoming individuals. At the same time, between the ages of three and four, children become moral beings: they develop the capacity to dissemble. A three-year-old who has hidden Snow White from the wicked witch will nevertheless tell the witch where Snow White is when she asks. A four-year-old will send the witch on a fruitless search somewhere else. Just as Adam and Eve become moral beings when they disobey God and lie about what has happened, so a child begins to differentiate herself from the world around her and take conscious responsibility for her actions.

Another key stage in the development of sexuality is, of course, adolescence, when there is rapid and sometimes overwhelming physical development. To negotiate this creatively, the adolescent needs to be both secure enough and free enough to detach himself to 'leave his father and mother' (Gen. 2.24) and form new relationships. It can be a time of great creativity as well as one of anxiety and confusion, when questions of orientation or gender identity come powerfully into play. It is often the time of a first explicitly sexual experience.

Sexuality, then, underlies our adult relationships and – for many people – having children. In these years many of us struggle with the ambiguity of erotic love. Erotic attraction is mysterious, and when we become aware of it we experience vulnerability as well as excitement. Erotic attraction opens up possibilities of delusion and truth:

- Delusion: we invest the other with our projections, desires and needs that are invisible to ourselves and eventually need to be recognized as our own.
- Truth: we may see through the externals to the precious, unique, made-in-the-image-of-God-ness of the other.

In a lasting relationship, there is a process of stripping away illusion, taking on the reality of the other person and allowing one's own reality to be seen. Beyond desire, lies the art of loving: allowing erotic attraction to mediate tenderness between people so that each enables the other to grow.

Learning to love as well as desire another person, to be together enough to be secure and separate enough to thrive as individuals and make room for children and others – all this is complicated and often painful to achieve. It requires us neither to exploit – using the other for our own purposes – nor to be exploited – handing ourselves over to the other – but for each to find in the other a subject rather than an object. In this way, as subject to subject, each is re-created and becomes more him- or herself.

One of the most common catastrophes in marriage is when this process becomes one-sided. One partner grows and matures, while the other continues locked into the original projections and refuses to accept that love and life change over time. For example, one or other partner may be unable to make room for children in the relationship and become jealous of the attention they receive, or what is for one partner a career, friendship or a hobby becomes a symbol of neglect for the other; equally one or other partner may take refuge in these things as an escape from the reality of the marriage.

However we live our sexuality – in partnership, alone or in community – the basic issues are the same. We need to find how we personally can 'make love' in a world sorely in need of love.

Sexuality does not, of course, come to an end as we enter into old age. Enjoying, understanding, healing – and living – our sexuality is a lifelong process. As we age and new generations come into being, our bodies go on changing, forcing us to come to terms with new dependencies and eventually to prepare for death. We learn to make way for new life. This does not mean we are no longer in need of intimacy, tenderness or even erotic love. As people age more slowly and live longer, there are many more 'late-flowering' relationships, which can be a great opportunity for both partners to harvest a lifetime of learning. There are also many more people in their seventies and even eighties who feel acutely the lack of a sexual partner in a way that would not usually have been expressed a few decades ago.

'Male and female' he created them

> So God created humankind in his image, in the image of God he created them; male and female he created them. (Gen. 1.27)

We are created in God's image, and being male and female is part of that image. In the history of the Church, it has not often been easy for Christians to accept themselves as fully sexual and gendered beings in the journey towards the Kingdom. Female imagery tends to be de-sexed (as in the virgin mother) or linked with the Fall (as in Eve). Yet there are plenty of female role models in the Bible who are three dimensional: gritty, beautiful, argumentative, truth seeking women such as Sarah, Rebecca, Rachel, Judith and Tamar – and there are the women who argue with Jesus and answer back, and who are accepted by him.

For men, too, so much has seeped into the Christian understanding of sexuality about control and renunciation that it is easy to forget the many robust images in the Old Testament and the New: Abraham who dares to bargain with God; Jacob who wrestles with the angel; David who commits murder to gain the woman he desires, and afterwards repents bitterly; Joseph who listens to the angel and protects Mary, his betrothed, from scandal; the apostles who drop everything to follow Christ and who struggle with their various rivalries, passions, triumphs and failures in order to understand and be faithful to him.

We also see sexual bonding with or without procreation in the Bible: Sarah and Abraham in the long years before the birth of Isaac; Jacob and Rebekah, the wife he loved for many years before he was allowed to marry her; Ruth and Boaz, Zachariah and Elizabeth, and so on.

Living in a gendered body affects both self-understanding and relating to others. While the majority of people feel at home in their gendered bodies this is less true of the gender roles assigned to them. All through our growing up we receive messages about what it is to be a boy or a girl. These messages may or may not fit well – or well enough – with our gendered embodiment. Sometimes they actually make it impossible to thrive as what we are. This is not only a matter of receiving love or affirmation from parents and family or being born a boy to parents who long for a girl or vice versa. Surrounding circumstances also play their part.

For example, Jenny's father was a housemaster in a boys' prep school, and she had three brothers. Her father and brothers, being energetic and sporty, were in their element. The only indication, however, of what it might mean to be a woman, was the life Jenny's mother led – managing the cooking, washing, baths and bedtimes for twenty or so boys. She did not find this fulfilling and struggled with chronic depression. By the time Jenny reached university, she herself was depressed and sought help. As she talked, it became clear that the very word 'woman' disgusted her: she could not value herself, because she could not value what she was. Gradually, as she reflected on her background, Jenny began to realize that she was valued as the girl in her family and as a talented young woman. Eventually she felt ready to risk her sexuality in a relationship with a man, though even so, she experienced this as such an invasion of her personal boundaries that she came close to breakdown. Her partner was loving and understanding, and over time she found ways to be herself and to say no as well as yes, with an authenticity that could be heard and responded to by both him and her family.

As with Jenny, sexual healing is usually very slow. The mind moves faster than the emotions (we can usually work out what is going on in a situation long before we can *feel* differently about it), and the body moves slower still. Our bodies carry all sorts of memories that we may not be conscious of. They need time to come to terms with change, such as when a person who is used to being treated roughly learns to relax when touched lovingly.

How we relate to each other as gendered beings presents a particular task for the Church as the body of Christ. We are told in Paul's letter to the Galatians that 'there is no longer male and female; for all of you are one in Christ Jesus' (3.28). This verse was picked up in the seventh century by Maximus the Confessor (580–662), who claims that the task of transcending gender has already been achieved in and by Christ:

> God-made-man has done away with the difference and division of nature into male and female (cf. Gal. 3.28) . . . First He united us in Himself by removing the difference between male and female, and instead of men and women, in whom above all this manner of division is beheld, he showed us as properly and truly to be simply human beings, thoroughly transfigured in accordance with him.[2]

Yet, if Christ has achieved this, what does it mean in practice? In the world in which we live, differences remain between men and women, physically, psychologically and spiritually. However much Christ transcends gender differences at a cosmic level, they still exist in the world we live in. In order, perhaps, to begin to live the reality of Galatians 3.28 we need to be asking:

- How do we recognize difference without exploitation?
- How do we allow ourselves to be alike without rivalry?
- What do we share as human beings?

In most contexts, including church ones, however, gender has become difficult to talk about, in part because of a huge residue of pain from people having been put in male or female straitjackets of expectations and assumptions. There is also a heightened sensitivity to the effect of gender stereotypes on work and family life.

In finding ways to understand and discuss the meaning of gender, we can identify four different ways in which we as a society tend to think about it:

---

2 Andrew Louth, 1996, *Maximus the Confessor*, London: Routledge, p. 159.

- **Man as primary: Woman as 'spare rib'** (Gen. 2.18–22). The man is the basic human being, and woman is brought into being to help him and alleviate his loneliness. In this model woman is defined in relation to man. She tends to be deprived of power in the public sphere (though she may wield considerable power in the private sphere).
- **Primary femininity.** This model treats the female as the basic human being. A biological process of separation begun in the womb continues into psychological life after birth when the man has to separate from the mother in order to forge his identity in a way that the woman does not. Equally, in contrast to being a 'spare rib', Woman may be seen as the crown of creation, reaching her apotheosis in Mary.
- **Complementarity.** As in Genesis 1.27, male–female differentiation is not explained: we are in the image of God. Man and woman are defined in relation to each other. This often includes a psychological understanding of each carrying the opposite sexuality unconsciously, finding it in the other to whom we are attracted.
- **Diffuse sexuality.** On this model, no one is defined by their gender. Anyone can fulfil any role, and physical sexual characteristics cannot be assumed to have any particular meaning for any particular person.

Each of these models has some ground in human experience and influences how we think about our own and the opposite sex. Each carries some potential for greater mutual understanding, as well as for denial of the other's reality, so it can be worth reflecting on which of them most closely resembles your own way of thinking and what it might mean to accommodate the others as possibilities.

Being transgendered or transexual

For most people questions about gender operate at a psychological or cultural level. There is a significant number of people, however, who have a sense of not being the gender that their body suggests that they are. This is a subject that many people find

deeply disturbing, and it is often relegated to the realms of enter-
tainment or sexual titillation. It is, however, a situation that is
increasingly recognized and acknowledged, and affects some
people at the very heart of their lives.

Transgendered sexuality exists on a broad spectrum. Most of us
can imagine what it might be like to be the opposite sex from our
own, and there are countless people who like to play with dressing up as or impersonating the opposite sex. For some people, this
has an erotic charge and may even be a strong desire during sex.
Further along the spectrum is a fundamental question of identity
and a powerful need to dress – at least some of the time – as a
woman if you are a man or a man if you are a woman. This is
what used to be known as transvestitism, but which tends now to
be called cross-dressing: the more ordinary language helps to take
it out of the realm of pathology into ordinary life.

For some, occasional cross-dressing is enough, but others need
to live at least part of the time as a member of the opposite sex as
well. Many people do this as a closely guarded secret, or change
identity in different situations.

While there are those who are at home with this kind of ambiguity, others find it does not work. They need to live full time as
a member of the opposite sex. And beyond these are the trans-
sexuals whose discomfort in their body is so acute that they opt
for surgery. There is no doubt that for some people gender reassignment through surgery releases them into the freedom to be
themselves. If someone is considering this, however, particularly
if they are young, it is essential that they are given the opportunity
to talk it through thoroughly with a psychologically trained professional. It can happen sometimes that the medical profession
cannot tolerate gender ambiguity and may advise surgery unnecessarily or prematurely.

Where you meet a transgendered person in a pastoral context,
you may also know husband, wife, children and other family
members, and you are likely to encounter strong feelings, especially at least in the initial stages of revelation. It is important
not to assume that spouses or partners will react in a particular
way: some find it easy to make the transition, while others resist
it to the point of divorce. Where it has been kept a secret by

the transgendered person, it may even be that having it out in the open improves the relationship. Janine was married to Colin for 20 years, before he confided in her that he longed to dress as a woman, and he began to live part-time as Corinna. For Janine, this meant a lot of tension went out of their relationship. 'Corinna is a much easier person than Colin,' she said a few months later.

Transgendered people may also rely heavily on your discretion: it may be for example that she or he has told some family members and not others, and it is important not to assume that because, say, a person's wife or husband knows, their children or parents also know. Pauline, for example, is a cross-dresser, who lives most of her life as a woman now she has retired and no longer goes out to work. She accepts that her children find this difficult and have not told her grandchildren about this. When she looks after the grandchildren, she does so in her original identity as Paul. For Pauline, this has been an amicable negotiation. Others are less fortunate. Harriet, another cross-dresser, whose male name is Henry, was rung up by her brother to say that their cousin had died. Harriet was sorry to hear this: she was fond of her cousin, who had been sympathetic to her transgendered way of life. 'When is the funeral?' she asked. There was a silence at the other end of the phone. Eventually her brother replied, 'It is on Tuesday at St John's at three.' He paused and then added, 'Henry is welcome to come. Harriet is not.' If someone has confided in you that they are living some of the time as a member of the opposite sex, be careful to check out who else knows about this.

When you yourself first encounter a transgendered person, you may need to spend some time getting used to your own reactions to meeting a woman in a man's body or a man in a woman's body – or to someone who has had gender reassignment surgery. It can take time to adjust – remember this is true of family and friends as well. For example, it was only in his forties that Stella's brother confided in her that he was living much of the time as a woman and was considering surgery. Although she did not express this to her brother directly, Stella was upset and angry, not least because this seemed to rewrite her own history as the female child in their family. It took a couple of years, before she was able to feel comfortable with her new 'sister', and even then she found the idea of a complete sex change very disturbing.

For any transgendered person, the journey to 'coming out' and finding others with whom to share experience is usually a lonely and vulnerable one. It is important to be aware that someone who is just beginning to identify in this way will probably be shedding a lifetime of secrecy and shame and may well be very needy, at least in the first year or two. Do not be afraid to encourage them and their family to seek professional support.

A common mistake is to assume that transgendered people are also homosexual. This is far from the case, and many transgendered people are happily married. One is about identity, the other about orientation.

Sexual orientation

Being uncertain about gender is a quite different thing from being attracted to members of one's own sex. Whatever your own views on same sex relationships, it is vital that you are aware of what your church teaches and clear about what you actually think and feel. Readers of this book will no doubt hold many different views, and it is not for us here to grapple with the Church's sexual ethics, but it is important to know what your own views are and what you found them on.

One of the difficulties in incorporating homosexual orientation into the Church's understanding is that traditional Church teaching assumes a procreational ethic, based on so-called natural law. God created male and female and the object of sexual relationships between them is to 'be fruitful and multiply' (Gen. 8.17). On the other hand, homosexual orientation exists in a proportion of the population across all cultures and even in the animal world, so natural law is often seen as a dubious basis on which to assume just what is 'normal' sexual behaviour.

Another factor is that same sex orientation is itself a relatively recent concept. Until quite recently, sexual ethics in church and society were concerned with particular acts: there was no concept of orientation as part of the identity of an individual. On this view, we are all subject to the same temptations and identity does not come into it.

It was only in 1967 that same sex relationships became legal in Britain. Nevertheless, same sex orientation was still widely considered a mental disorder, and it was only removed from the American Psychiatric Association's diagnostic manual in 1977. Today, orientation towards same sex relationships tends to be part of how we understand sexual identity – though there are still people, in and out of the Church, who see it as an illness.

It seems quite clear that while there are people who would never be attracted to the same sex, and others who would never be attracted to the opposite sex, most people have a measure of bisexuality in their make-up. That is, they can be attracted in an erotic way to members of the same and opposite sex, although they may primarily be attracted to one or the other. Some people have no trouble in acknowledging this – others find it disturbing.

Attraction to the same sex can be a question of circumstances. If you are in a prison or a school, where there are no members of the opposite sex, and your hormones are active, there is more likelihood that you will be attracted to members of your own sex. For some people, too, same sex attraction is a developmental phase: a stage on the way to separating from the family of origin and forging a sexual identity. Many people have a first relationship with someone of the same sex, but spend the rest of their lives in heterosexual relationships.

This does not mean, however, that homosexuality is simply a developmental phase or can be 'cured' by therapy or other means. There are countless people who from an early age know themselves to be primarily attracted to the same sex. This discovery is rarely free from anxiety even in the most liberal circumstances, and telling other people is almost always risky. At the age of 14, Tony realized he was gay, and he was impressed when a sixth-former came out, and was accepted by his year group. Encouraged, Tony decided he too would come out. What he had not realized was that the sixth-former had a well established reputation in other spheres and was also about to leave the school. He could 'afford' to come out. Tony was less well-placed and was also stuck at school for a further three years, for most of which he was bullied because of his homosexual identity.

Nevertheless, society in general at least appears more tolerant than the churches, whose attitude can be simply bewildering for people whether they themselves are gay or straight. The fundamental problem that faces the gay Christian as he or she grows up is expressed clearly by the Roman Catholic priest and theologian, James Alison:

> I was told that my same-sex orientation was the fruit of original sin. The explanation was proffered as something which justified severe control and which seemed to call for dramatic hatred of self in order to be good. But this, too, is puzzling: why was something [sexual desire] which was held to have affected all people equally since Adam to be understood as justifying the massive 'no' which Christian people spoke to the depth of my being, when it implied no comparable depth of 'no' to the lives of my heterosexual contemporaries?[3]

This 'no' is so powerful, and so difficult to keep to in practice that it often leads to what is also widely perceived as hypocrisy where clergy and others say one thing and do another, as described in Bernard Lynch's outspoken book about his own experience as a Catholic priest.[4] His is a dramatic story, but the 'double standard' is encountered at many levels. A typical story is that of Alex, a gay man in a long-term partnership who wanted to offer himself to train for ordination in the Anglican Church. After talks over several months with a Diocesan Director of Ordinands they agreed it was time for him to go to a selection conference. 'What should I say if they ask about my sexuality?' he asked. 'Just lie,' she replied cheerfully. This marked the end of Alex's relationship with the Church. 'I don't mind them objecting to my being gay,' he said, 'but I could not stomach the idea that they should expect me to lie about who I am.'

Today in this country, civil partnerships have become the norm for same sex couples, who wish to stay together in a faithful

---

3 James Alison, 1998, *The Joy of Being Wrong: Original Sin through Easter Eyes*, New York: Crossroad, p. 2.

4 Bernhard Lynch, 2012, *If it Wasn't Love: A Journal about Sex, Death and God*, Alresford: Circle Books.

relationship, while there is no official way for the Church to bless this. There are still, however, many parts of society – as well as churches – where homosexuality is more or less unacceptable and where there is risk of rejection or even violence. Even where this is not the case, families and friends of someone who reveals him or herself as gay may have strong feelings about it. Again, as pastor, you may be called upon to accommodate many different viewpoints and reactions, and the more aware you are of your own the more useful you can be. You do not have to agree with people – but you do need to be secure enough in yourself to allow them to disagree with you.

Going it alone

The churches are increasingly having to face up to the fact that whatever their teaching may be about marriage and family life, more and more people do not live in traditional marriages. Less than half the domestic units in this country are 'nuclear' families. More and more people are living alone or as single parents, and there are growing numbers of 'informal' families: more or less loosely clustered communities who often have intimate arrangements around child care, finances, cars, etc. When the traditional family declines, people create new forms of family life.

Nevertheless, most of us spend a proportion of our adult lives living alone. For some people this is a choice (and may be a question of vocation), but for many others it is an unwelcome necessity. Whatever the reason, it is important to remember that solitude does not necessarily mean loneliness and vice versa.

Solitude is grounded in the capacity to be alone, which is a strong indicator of mental well-being. It looks outwards and inwards and is aware of inner resources and limitations. Loneliness, on the other hand, is an experience of separateness, emptiness and alienation that leaves us feeling unhappy, unfulfilled and anxious. Whether we live alone or with others we all move in and out of these states, but the person who lives alone is more exposed to loneliness. For all its difficulties family life in its various forms is a great buffer against existential angst. On the other hand living alone gives you freedom and time that can seem enviable to people living in families. Yet, singleness does not release us from the requirements of relationship, any more than family life releases us from the requirement to be oneself.

In church communities, as in demanding families, it is often assumed that a single person is available to fill the gaps in a way that a married person is not – and that they should be grateful to be included: Pat, who has a family, cannot be expected to join the PCC, while June, who does not, has nothing else to do – disregarding the fact that June not only has a job, but also does her own shopping and housework and needs time to recharge her batteries. It is easy to feel – and be – exploited. Jeffrey was a young single man with a talent for producing topical Power Point presentations which enlivened the services at his church and which the vicar loved and wanted regularly. 'It was great at first – I felt special – but I ended up feeling used. I had a full-time job, and no one cared that I was just knocking myself out keeping up with all this stuff.'[5]

The same can happen to widowed and divorced people. Jill, who had been happily married for 30 years, nursed her husband through a long illness, before he died. Within a few months of his death, the vicar came round to ask what work she would like to do in the parish, now she was alone. 'I am sure he meant well,' she said, 'but I am living alone for the first time in a very long time. Though I miss Gerald terribly, I now have time to do all the things I could not do while he was ill – and I am not ready to start looking after other people.'

It is also the case that single people often find that other community members misunderstand their boundaries when it comes to touch – or even sexual advances. People vary enormously in how they experience simple physical intimacy such as a handshake, a hug, a peck on the cheek or exchanging the Peace during the Eucharist. For some, this contact may be welcome, while for others it can be an invasion of personal space. When it comes to sex, it is often assumed that a single person either knows nothing – or must be desperate for a sexual rela-

---

5 Quoted in Jessica Rose, 2009, *Church on Trial*, London: Darton, Longman and Todd, p. 70.

tionship. Even today, there is often an assumption that any relationship is better than none, though this is far from the truth. As a single person, you may find your space invaded, or that you are treated as a threat to other people's relationships. It is still the case that many couples avoid inviting single people to meals and social events.

This is sad, since church communities have great potential for single and married people to mix with each other in ways that are not often possible elsewhere. We tend, nevertheless, to divide them up – having groups and conferences for married people separately from single people. Yet, they have much to learn from each other and to envy in each other. Exchanging experiences can help us to respect the differences and build bridges so that each can widen their horizons.

Talking about sexuality

When it comes to talking about sexuality, Bob Whorton, a hospice chaplain, describes an experience that will be familiar to many people:

> The family I grew up in was not always comfortable about touch and *bodies*. From the Church I received the message that sex outside marriage was sinful . . . And as a young teenager in the permissive 1960s I was a great testament to the teaching of depth psychology – that what we cannot tolerate we push into the unconscious . . . so part of my journey towards healing has involved befriending my sexuality.[6]

It is true that sexuality is talked about much more openly today than it was 50 years ago. This does not necessarily make it easier to talk personally at a deep level. To do so means taking risks and makes us vulnerable on both sides of the conversation. Here we offer a few guidelines for pastors who find themselves sharing with people on matters of sexuality.

---

6 Bob Whorton, 2011, *Reflective Caring: Imaginative Listening to Pastoral Experience*, London: SPCK, p. 76.

- Be aware of your own situation in relation to that of the person you are talking with. You may be in a happy and settled relationship or finding meaning in celibacy, while they may feel a terrible emptiness where a relationship should be or suffering in a bad marriage. In either case, it is unlikely to help if you extol the freedom and opportunities of the single state or the ideals and joys of married life. Equally, if you are going through a bad time, be aware that it is not like this for everyone.

- Remember that if you are unhappy with your own sexuality or with your life situation, this makes you vulnerable. Jack was single and rather lonely for the first few years of his ministry and then embarked on a deeply satisfying marriage. 'When I did not have what I have now,' he said, 'it was in some ways much easier to support people in their loneliness or in difficult relationships – perhaps because I was more easily able to accept that this was what life was like. Now I have higher expectations – for myself and others.'

- Be aware that very often less is more. To be heard and accepted is often all that is needed – though do make it clear that you *have* heard. In his memoir, *Leaving Alexandria*, Richard Holloway writes about his long and painful struggles over masturbation, when he was being educated for the priesthood. He describes his overwhelming shame and dread of Confession – but also the silence with which his confession was received:

As far as human anguish goes it was at the lower end of the spectrum, but it was pain enough, and it left a shadow. I have often wished I had met someone then, maybe someone like the priest I became later, who could have told me to relax, that it was natural, just don't turn it into a full time occupation.[7]

- Be sensitive to the fact that if someone has shared something very personal with you, they may feel vulnerable

---

7 Richard Holloway, 2012, *Leaving Alexandria: A Memoir of Faith and Doubt*, Edinburgh/London: Canongate Press, p. 74.

the next time you meet. Let *them* decide whether to speak about it again.

- Never forget the context in which you have received a confidence and that you are not at liberty to bring it up elsewhere. This may sound obvious, but it is astonishing how many people have cringed in their pew while the vicar uses their private dilemma – anonymously of course – as the subject of a sermon.

- Beware of prurient interest – your own. You may find what someone has told you extremely interesting and want to follow it up, but they may have said all they want to say to you. Make it clear you are available, but do not push the agenda.

- It helps to start from what is, so make sure you know what the Church says about questions of sexuality and also where you yourself stand in relation to those things. There may be things in Church teaching that you yourself find hard to live with. For example, there are many clergy who struggle with the ruling in the Roman Catholic Church that debars a divorced person who remarries from communion.

- Remember that very often what upsets people is not so much the rules required by the Church but the hypocrisy with which they are treated by those in authority.

- Try to combine an accepting attitude with honesty. People may well tell you things that make you feel uncomfortable or even disgust you. It may sometimes be important to be able to say, 'I personally find it hard to go along with that', or suggest that you talk further when you have had some time to reflect.

- If you do feel uncomfortable and go on doing so, it is possible that you are being recruited to the other person's inner world in a way that is not helpful for either of you. It is also possible it is touching on some unresolved problem of your own. Check the situation out with someone you can trust.

- Remember that just as spirituality cannot bypass sexuality, so true acceptance cannot bypass shock. If something shocks you, listen to the shock and weigh it up. It may be telling you that something appalling is happening, or it may be telling you that you are meeting a situation of which you have no experience, but which is in itself not damaging – or which is closer to you than you would wish. Check it out with other people. Learn the importance of time and adjustment in yourself, and in the friends and families of the person concerned.

- Do not assume that because someone has reached old age they no longer have sexual needs. A person who is widowed or loses a partner in those years may still experience extreme sexual loneliness as well as other aspects of bereavement.

6

Sexuality (2):
Some Darker Aspects of Sexuality

In this chapter, we will briefly explore sexuality and power in pastoral relationships, before going on to look at some darker aspects of sexuality, where its relational aspect is lost:

- Sexual compulsion and victimization.
- Sadism and masochism.
- Violence in the home.
- Some consequences of the sexual abuse of children.

Sexuality and power in pastoral relationships

In pastoral work, it is a common – but highly dangerous – temptation to underrate or ignore the power of sexuality. Yet this power has great healing potential. Sexuality opens us up to new possibilities of relationship and self-understanding and brings us into communion with the creative power of God, of which having children is only one aspect. As Fynn's Anna puts it, 'It puts seeds in your heart and new things come.'[1] As pastoral carers, we participate in the healing power of Christ, and those we care for are also powerful: they carry our sense of being a good pastor, and this can be sustaining and help us grow.

At the same time, however, pastoral care begets intimacy and intimacy often begets responses in ourselves and others that we would prefer not to exist. This is inevitable because of the powerful

---

1 Fynn, 1974, *Mister God, This is Anna*, London: Harper Collins, p. 86.

projections that people carry for each other in helping situations. Each projects on to the other their own unconscious associations, expectations, hopes and fears. This is neither a bad thing nor a good thing: it just is. But it can be particularly risky for pastoral workers, who often work alone with minimal supervision, in their own and other people's homes, and who may have a strong personal investment in their role. To be able to acknowledge what is going on is the first step to recovery.

For example, Steve, a young curate in a busy suburban parish began visiting Michael, an elderly artist who, like many creative people, suffered from bipolar disorder. When Michael was down, he relied heavily on being able to talk to people and even share his thoughts of suicide. These bouts of depression would eventually lift, and Michael would find new energy for his work. His mood often plummeted on completion of a project.

Steve became very attached to Michael during these visits, in which Michael shared openly with him about his feelings of despair and struggles with faith. When the time approached for Steve to move on to a new parish, he realized that he was very upset about leaving Michael. He had what he could describe as a longing for the times he spent sitting with Michael at his home, which was not a sexual longing but was intense, and he did not know how to say goodbye to him. He was sometimes tempted to say nothing at all.

As Steve talked this over with a trusted friend, he began to see links between Michael and his own father, who had committed suicide when Steve was 14. In Michael he had found an older man who had managed *not* to kill himself and who was able to share his feelings in a way that Steve's father never had. He realized that Michael had restored something of his own father to him and was able to tell Michael that he would miss him. Michael, too, was able to affirm how Steve had helped him, and they were able to say a sincere and mutual goodbye to each other.

In his book, *Sex in the Forbidden Zone*, Peter Rutter argues that there is always an element of self-deception in professional relationships.[2] He maps out ways in which men in authority, including

---

2 Peter Rutter, 1989, *Sex in the Forbidden Zone*, New York: Ballantine Books.

clergy and therapists, fall into their own wounds, when it comes to intimacy. What he has to say is, of course, largely applicable also to women and to same sex relationships. He shows how, as the boundaries become loose in a healing relationship, the very potential for healing can turn impossibly destructive.

Nevertheless, we should not forget the healing power of sexuality. When we refuse to act on our own desire or to make use of another person's, the wounds that were at the root of the desire can sometimes be healed. If this healing is to come, it is essential to maintain boundaries lovingly, acknowledging the other as a true person, neither renounced nor mistrusted nor exploited. Shared faith and the ritual of the community can help to sustain this.

For example, Alison became seriously ill in her forties, when she recovered buried memories of sexual abuse when she was a small child. She was the daughter of a priest, who had died some years before, as had her mother, and she had a strong affection for Graham, her parish priest and his wife. At some level they were substitute parents for her.

When Alison's memories surfaced, she realized that her own father had been unable to face it and ignored what happened to her: feelings of abandonment that she had experienced then came up and were transferred to Graham, making her very needy for a while. During this time, Graham was caring and available, while maintaining firm boundaries. In particular, he was careful not to touch Alison, though there were times when he could sense that she very much wanted this.

Years later, Alison said that one of the most healing things for her in that time was that she knew that Graham cared for her, but also that he knew exactly where his boundaries were and that he would not cross them. She may have longed at the time for him to hug or hold her, but what she needed was loving restraint in order to get her own boundaries back in place. In due course – but not until he was sure she was well on the way to recovery – Graham anointed Alison, and also held a prayer service for her dead father, explicitly bringing her wounds for spiritual as well as psychological healing.

Graham was fortunate to be happily married, so, although he found Alison attractive, the situation was well under his control.

All too often this is not the case: the longing reaches out to a lonely place in the pastor, and the struggle to maintain the healing power of love without giving into it can be extremely tough.

Where desire is at work, any one of us can get caught up in a mythology of redemption: only I can understand so-and-so and bring him – or her – in from the cold; if only I had someone like this to work with/talk with/live with, I would be a different person. Tragically, we often try to suppress the feelings until they have become so powerful that the only way out is a brutal renunciation. The other is treated as a child, there is no goodbye, and she or he can be left feeling not only abandoned but dangerous and undesirable.

Sexual compulsion and victimization

We are told, 'Let us love one another, for love is from God' (1 John 4.7). For much of the time, loving is a struggle – not only to come to terms with the way we ourselves are challenged and changed by others, but also to allow the other to be a subject in their own right, not an object of our own projections and desires.

In its darker aspects, sexuality becomes divorced from love and even drives us apart rather than bringing us closer together. Far from embracing the other as subject, it turns them into an object, as when a boyfriend or girlfriend is more important as a status symbol than as a friend and companion. The journey into love is a long one, and we all have to learn as we go along, but we can also develop blocks on the way which make it very difficult to move forward. These blocks arise in part from the fears inherent in sexual relationships – fear of abandonment, of losing oneself, of losing one's freedom, of physical attack. And they also arise from our own histories.

Here we enter the realms of what is 'normal' and what is 'deviant' or 'perverse' in sexual behaviour. This is constantly under discussion and fiercely argued. The very words 'deviance' and 'perversion' are widely rejected in liberal circles and also defended by some groups to preserve a distinction between morality and sin.

The American psychoanalyst Robert J. Stoller argues in his book, *Perversion: The Erotic Form of Hatred*, that both these stances are wrong and seeks to find the common factor in sexual perversion, 'regardless of the specific behaviours that make one perversion different from another'.[3] Where Stoller's ideas are useful for our purposes is that he claims that the 'defining factor' in perversion is hostility. It objectifies rather than subjectifies the other. Fantasy recruits others to the inner theatre of the mind, whether or not it is acted out, and has a compulsive quality linked to early experience:

> From Freud on, it has been said that precocious excitement contributes to perversion. I would agree, but only – as must usually be the case – when there has been too much stimulation and too little discharge or severe guilt. These will then be sensed as traumatic and be transformed via the magic of the perverse ritual into a successful venture.[4]

By 'too much stimulation' is meant here an experience that is too highly charged to be understood or absorbed by the child; and 'too little discharge' that the child has not been able to process the experience and let it go. Guilt may result from this or from further specific interventions by adults or other children.

In the following section, we will take one particular strand of so-called perversion, sadism and masochism, and look at how these are played out in the relationship between aggressor and victim – something that is far from obvious until we look closely. On Stoller's model, the masochist is acting out unconscious hostility just as much as the sadist.

The veiled hostility that lies in sadomasochistic relationships is a widespread feature of human relating and operates at a psychological as well as a sexual level.

This subject is also relevant for us in order to distinguish sadomasochism from violence perpetrated by one person against another, either between adults or in the sexual abuse of children.

---

3 R. J. Stoller, 1986, *Perversion: The Erotic Form of Hatred*, London: Karnac, p. xi.
4 Stoller, *Perversion*, p. 7.

Sadism and masochism

We tend to think of sadism and masochism as belonging in specialist night clubs and brothels, but they are usually present in some form in all sexual relationships and influence our behaviour in many ways. Where they become perverse is where they become predominant or concrete, or the need for fantasy takes over from intimacy.

In sexual terms, sadism has the specific quality of excitement attached to inflicting pain and fantasies of that. Fantasy and practice may be very sophisticated, and in this sense is closer to torture or torment than lashing out in uncontrolled anger: 'carefully regulated cruelties'.[5] The masochist may be terrified of pain, but finds sexual excitement in the idea of it, especially, again, when inflicted in a highly ritualized – and therefore controlled – way. Both sadistic and masochistic fantasies often go with a profound sense of shame. A person who has them may well say, 'I hate people being hurt and that I get excited by these fantasies', but still the fantasies keep coming.

In both sadism and masochism, fantasy life is crucial to sexual release, and the presence of the sexual partner may become secondary or even irrelevant. As Stoller puts it, '[They] deal with their partners as if the others were not real people but rather puppets to be manipulated on the stage.'[6]

As Stoller argues, we can often find the roots of sexual fantasy in childhood trauma and frustration:

In the perverse act, one endlessly relives the traumatic or frustrating situation that started the process, but now the outcome is marvellous, not awful, for not only does one escape the threat, but finally immense sexual gratification is attached to the consummation.[7]

People caught up in their own sexual fantasies rarely understand how the fantasy is constructed: the actual events may not even be remembered – they only know that the fantasy is essential to a sexual experience and can become completely compelling.

---

5 Doris Lessing, 1996, *Love Again*, London: Penguin, 2006, p. 201.
6 Stoller, *Perversion*, p. 105.
7 Stoller, *Perversion*, p. 105.

For example, throughout adolescence and adult life, Richard had found it hard to get sexually aroused without using some form of a particular fantasy that emerged in his mind as he reached puberty: that he is accused of a crime he has not committed; is sent to wait for punishment; agrees to suffer so many strokes of the cane and bears the pain heroically. As time went on, this fantasy became more and more compelling for him, so that he felt a frequent and urgent need to release himself sexually through it, with or without his wife. He could never bring himself to confide any of this in her. She simply experienced that at a certain point in their lovemaking he seemed detached as though his mind was elsewhere, and she became frightened that he was in love with someone else.

Richard sought help, because he loved his wife and realized that his 'absence' during sex was disturbing for her. The only thing he could relate to the fantasy from his early experience was a dim memory that his father had once been very angry and had beaten him, but he could remember no details of it, nor could he remember the pain of being punished. He had always assumed that his father had behaved reasonably, but as he explored the memory of the incident, he realized that his father's anger and the beating he had received had been sudden and uncontrolled. The effect was shattering and humiliating as well as horribly painful, and even as an adult he found it hard to take in what had been done to him. His mind still refused to let the memory into consciousness.

He was able to see, however, that the fantasy was a way of putting some kind of boundary around the experience, so that he could, in a sense, control what was done to him and, even more importantly, by bearing it heroically, 'triumph' over his father's anger. Realizing this was the beginning of being able – over months and years – gradually to let go of the fantasy and be more present in lovemaking with his wife.

In Richard's case, a punishment had amounted to a sudden attack, which he could not assimilate. Sometimes masochistic fantasies arise out of a situation, where there has been some other kind of catastrophe that has not met with an adequate response: whatever was wrong seems to spread out into infinity, and the sexual fantasy or acting out can be a way of handling the chaos. If you make a boundary in the form of physical pain – even if it is only in your head – at least you know where you are. The hurting tells you that you exist, that you are in your skin, where you end and the outside world begins. In this way, it can be the first step to survival – but, as with Richard, it may become so essential to survival that it becomes an end in itself.

This, too, is what goes on in some forms of self-harm: the mental pain is such that the physical pain of, for example, hitting or cutting oneself is a needed distraction and can become addictive. In the gratification, there is also an element of sadism, even if that sadism is turned against oneself. It is a way of blocking out the other – and may of course be a necessary survival mechanism.

Although masochism is an aspect of sexuality, sexual fantasy or acting out is only one expression of it. It also includes finding pleasure, relief or satisfaction, which may or may not be sexual pleasure, in pain or humiliation, either in reality or fantasy and a search for oblivion.[8]

In daily life, masochism is akin to what is known as 'passive aggression': hostility expressed, for example, by a heavy sigh while a person does exactly what they are asked to do and clearly does not want to. The masochist may become addicted to being the one who is always working longer hours than anyone else, carrying the extra burden, being the one who is put upon. Pain can be very protective: paradoxically the place where we are in pain becomes the safe place and we refuse to leave it because it somehow defines us. It tells us that we are good and the others are falling short.

The search for oblivion can take the form of letting another person take over your life. Delegating self-responsibility to another can be mistaken for love, and this can operate on many levels. A common manifestation is when there is an assumption that one member of the household will dictate the mood of the household, govern the dietary habits of the whole family, always take over the TV remote control . . . The masochistic tendency does not challenge this, and calls the lack of challenge love. If you feel you do not deserve a life it is easier to live someone else's.

Inherent in masochism is an inverted sadism, which is in fact a desperate effort to control or appease or simply put in the wrong

---

8 In his 1920 essay, 'Beyond the Pleasure Principle', Freud made a connection between masochism and death wish.

someone who is perceived as a threat. To allow – or even force – someone to treat us badly can be a very hostile thing to do. Stoller argues that masochism is an unconscious attempt to get back at someone who has at some time or other subjected us to an intolerable humiliation or pain. Some men and women constantly choose partners who humiliate or abandon them:

> These people have lusciously martyrish gratifications such as 'they'll-be-sorry-when-I'm gone', or 'at-least-God-loves-me', or 'contrast-my-saintliness-with-those-who-hurt-me' which convert the physical victim into psychological victor over his tormentor; the act is performed before a fantasied audience whose function is to recognize that the sadistic partner is a brute.[9]

This is not to say that there is no such thing as genuine victimization of one person by another, or that there are no innocent victims of other people's aggression. As Simone Weil (1909–43) says, 'The innocent victim knows the truth about his executioner: the executioner does not know it'.[10] All too often, however, there is buried anger at the heart of masochism.

In his book, *Holiness*, Donald Nicholl (1923–97) describes a sense of unease when talking with some married couples:

> In almost all cases of marital breakdown, I had an uneasy feeling that one or other of the partners seemed to put up with more from the other than he or she should have done. But it was difficult for me to ground this feeling since the 'suffering' partner so very often appeared to be noble and to be putting up with the other partner's behaviour quite heroically.[11]

Nicholl sometimes found himself seriously angry with the wronged partner: to allow oneself to be treated in this way was an insult to humanity – not just that person's business but everyone's. He goes

9 Stoller, *Perversion*, p. 58.
10 Simone Weil, 1992, *Gravity and Grace*, London: Routledge, p. 64.
11 Donald Nicholl, 1981, *Holiness*, London: Darton, Longman and Todd, p. 52.

on to quote the Jewish tradition: 'If I am here, the whole of mankind is here' – not, as he says, 'an arrogant statement, but a sober formulation of a basic truth'. Allowing ourselves to be badly treated, as Erich Fromm has also noted, can be a way of neatly avoiding responsibility. It is not difficult to give up what we never had, and quite a different thing from making a conscious choice to accept suffering that is inevitable or necessary. Whichever partner in the relationship is allowing the other to treat them as less than a person has a responsibility to challenge the abuse – otherwise they are also treating the other as less than a person.

Since suffering is so deeply embedded in the Christian story, it is worth thinking about how we understand that – and exploring it with other people. Masochism is sometimes identified as the shadow side of a capacity for worship. In her book, *Masochism: a Jungian View*, Lynn Cowan argues that it is a psychological reality in human beings and discusses how it can be acknowledged and harnessed in spirituality and a capacity for submission to God.[12] In Chapter 4, we quoted Hadjewich's seven names of love which go to the heart of the ambiguity of mystical experience and ecstasy, and she herself speaks of 'Love, whose tender care enlarges our wounds'.[13]

Nevertheless, masochism feeds on guilt, and all too often manifests itself in a fixation on the Passion and Crucifixion that does not take the resurrection into account. Of course we need to enter deeply into Christ's suffering and death, but always in the light of its redemptive movement towards resurrection, not as an end in itself. Many of us are very good at identifying with Christ's suffering but find it much more difficult to be receptive to Christ's healing power, to the moment that C. S. Lewis describes in *The Lion, the Witch and the Wardrobe* as when death itself starts working backwards.

For example, Siobhan was a committed church member, assiduous in helping other people, but often depressed, and she tended to get caught up in destructive relationships. Every Holy

---

12 Lynn Cowan, 1982/1990, *Masochism: A Jungian View*, Dallas, TX: Spring Publications.

13 *Hadjewich: The Complete Works*, The Classics of Western Spirituality, Ramsey, NJ: Paulist Press, 1980, p. 356.

Week, as the story progressed, she became increasingly over-whelmed by guilt, and when Easter came she stayed away, over-whelmed with misery. One year, she resolved to spend Easter morning at home, reading and meditating on the resurrection parts of all four Gospels. She found her attention caught by the women who went to the tomb. Since she herself was drawn to death and dying, she could easily identify with their desire to anoint the body of Jesus.

She also noticed that this story was told in a matter of fact way: 'They came to the tomb taking the spices that they had prepared' (Luke 24.1). This struck her as significant. 'It suddenly occurred to me,' she said, 'that they were not making a big deal of it. This terrible thing had happened to someone they loved so they did what you always did in those days – kept the ritual going.' In the garden, she then saw, the angel asked them a question that also hit home, 'Why do you look for the living among the dead?' (Luke 24.5). 'It really hit me between the eyes,' she said. 'That's what I am doing all the time. I don't notice what's alive around me because I am always drawn to death.' For Siobhan this was a turning point in beginning to value herself and shed the weight of guilt she carried.

A person who is inclined to masochism will try to invest clergy and other pastoral workers with too much power. Affirmation of the person without colluding by abusing the power they try to give you – even sometimes pointing out that you do not want that power – can be an effective pastoral intervention. It is all part of developing mutuality. If we are to be truly known, we have to accept being known as neither wholly good or wholly bad. Peter betrayed Jesus, and when he became aware of it he 'went out and wept bitterly' (Luke 22.62). His grief had nothing luxuriant about it: it was a bitter grief. You could say that he was able to experi-ence and come through that grief, because he could recognize and accept Jesus's love, which would survive even this betrayal. Judas on the other hand, who also betrayed Jesus in a much more con-crete way, killed himself. He could not receive the love that had been offered.

Violence in the home

It is crucial to distinguish between sadism and masochism as tendencies within human sexuality and violence acted out in the home. This is an ever increasing problem – men attacking women, women attacking men (by some estimates up to 40 per cent of adult to adult attacks), adults attacking children, children (particularly adolescents) attacking parents. Here we will be mainly concerned with violence between adults, though any violence in the home affects children, and it is strongly correlated with abuse of one sort or another.

Physical violence is real, frightening and damaging. It is an abuse of power that also takes place emotionally and verbally. Church contexts are far from exempt: sadly the power structures of the Church are all too often acted out in the home. Violence takes place right across society, as well as in church congregations, where it is usually expertly concealed – and often ignored or covered up if discovered.

The Government definition of domestic violence is broad:

> Any incident of threatening behaviour, violence or abuse (psychological, physical, sexual, financial or emotional) between adults who are or have been intimate partners or family members, regardless of gender or sexuality.[14]

Violence in the home is rarely a one-off incident: usually there is a pattern of behaviour, whereby one person tries to control another, and over time it tends to get worse rather than better.

People often say of a violent family member, 'She/he can't help it' or 'loses control.' Yet more often than not:

- The violence is specific to a particular victim, and does not extend to other situations such as work – or the PCC.
- She or he is able to stop and behave normally, if the police arrive or the doorbell rings.

---

14 www.domesticviolencelondon.nhs.uk/1-what-is-domestic-violence-/1-definition.html.

- Injuries are likely to be in places where others cannot see them.
- She or he may damage other people's possessions but rarely his or her own.

Once a pattern of physical or verbal violence has set in to a relationship, it is extremely hard to break. Many people stay with violent partners because of a genuine and rational fear of persecution if they leave, because they do not have anywhere else to go or the money to go there, or because they do not see how they can support their children alone. It helps to be able to say an internal and external 'no' to violence, but it is not guarantee of success.

There are three psychological features common to violent behaviour:

- dualistic thinking,
- anxiety,
- splitting in order to avoid anxiety.

We are born into a world full of opposites, and we very quickly learn to differentiate between them. Most of us can integrate them to some extent, and tolerate a degree of ambivalence between opposites like good and bad. The greater the threat, however, the more we are inclined to split our world into opposite 'sides'. This way of thinking is reinforced all the time in institutions, the media and family prohibitions, none of which are inclined to subtlety. We tend to divide people up, for example, into:

Good	Bad
On my side	Not on my side
Powerful	Powerless

While the world is ordered in this way, we can protect ourselves reasonably well because we know what to allow and what to avoid, what to encourage and what to destroy. However, most of us discover that we and others are not easily categorized in this way.

We like to think that 'I love you' means only positive things. Of course, it is a positive statement, but unless it is to turn into another dualism – love versus hate – we have to accept that for most of us loving someone also includes:

- being angry when you do not conform to my idea of what I would like you to be,
- seeing myself in you and finding that difficult,
- betraying and being betrayed because we trust each other,
- finding it hard to forgive,
- being jealous, envious, possessive,
- being anxious and angry when we seem to be too separate.

These are difficult things to live with, but they have to be lived with if the 'either – or' that splits people apart is to become a 'both-and' that holds people together. 'Either–or' leads all too easily to the common cycle of violence shown in Table 1.

Table 1: The cycle of violence

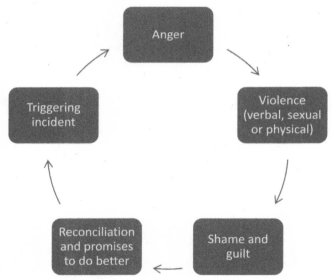

The psychotherapist Adam Jukes has worked extensively with men who batter their female partners and is critical of models that implicitly blame women as the cause of male violence – as mothers who produce violent sons or as women addicted to masochistic behaviour ('women who love too much').[15] We do not, argues Jukes, blame a bank for being robbed. The problem is the violence and the person committing violence has to take responsibility for it.[16]

Equally important in Jukes' analysis is that women do not have equal power with men in social, economic and political terms – and this is also true physically. Some traditional models suggest that women provoke or collude in violence, while Jukes's work shows that violence often continues however the victim adapts her behaviour. Making lists of trigger events does not help: the list is endless and changes from day to day.

Jukes argues that we are all suffering from a deep split in the psyche related to failure in our early dependency. This is akin to separation anxiety: a mixture of primary dread of annihilation, fragmentation, grief and rage. The experience of it is potentially annihilating. Jukes suggests that this exists in all of us, but is expressed differently in women and men. Rage and aggression are central to it in both sexes, but the social and cultural shaping of gender identity often precludes overt violence as an expression for women (women do not normally start wars or revolutions).

Where men are violent towards women, all the terror of abandonment is projected on to the feminine other – and being male means that he can dissociate himself from her, so that there is no sense of her as a real person. When his authority and/or sense of control are challenged, he feels helpless and vulnerable. He experiences such confusion that he is unable to differentiate his feelings. All he experiences is threat – so he attacks.

What Jukes does, in the particular case of men being violent towards women, is to insist that violent men take responsibility for their own violence rather than blame the woman as the cause of it. He also criticizes ways in which society tolerates treatment of women that feeds the possibility of violence.

Unfortunately, this is still an aspect of church life. The interpretation of the Fall as Eve's fault and some of the sayings in the

---

15 Robin Norwood, 2007, *Women who Love Too Much*, London: Arrow Books.

16 A. Jukes, 1993, 'Violence, Helplessness Vulnerability and Male Sexuality', *Free Associations* 4:1, p. 25.

Epistles are used – or abused – to take a similar line. A common example is the so-called 'severed head fallacy' where Ephesians 5.22 ('Wives be subject to your husbands as to the Lord for the husband is the head of the wife just as Christ is the head of the Church . . .') is quoted without reference to the following passage where it is said that Christ gave himself for the Church and nourishes and cares for it. On this basis women are still even today often encouraged to 'sacrifice' themselves to abusive husbands, feeding any masochistic tendency there may be and making it difficult to take a stand against it or to separate herself from it.

Where men suffer violence from women, they too can find it hard to break out of a perceived Christian ideal of who they should be.

Violence in pastoral situations

In any church community you will find anger and violence. A woman or man who is violent in private may have – and convince others of – an unrealistically good self-image which pushes any badness deep down to a place where it is only triggered by intimate relationship. It then breaks out in verbal, emotional or physical abuse.

Where there is physical violence, the issues are clear cut. It should not be tolerated. In emotional and psychological violence – or bullying – the question of how to respond can be much more complicated.

For example, Nina had been married for 15 years to Robert, who was often loving and sensitive but who was given to huge outbursts of anger followed by days of angry sulking. The whole family were regular churchgoers, and both Nina and Robert held responsible positions in parish life. In relationship counselling, they were advised that Robert needed to deal with his anger, and he went on an anger management course – but nothing changed. Nina sought counselling, but terminated it, when the counsellor suggested she should take the children and leave. She was unhappy in her marriage, but she still believed in the vows she had made.

Situations like this are often intransigent, and this one weighed heavily on Jonathan, their parish priest. He respected Nina's choice, but what he saw of the marriage distressed him. He realized that he longed to rescue Nina and was attracted to her, though as a pastor he had a duty of care to the whole family. He tried to encourage Robert to seek further help, and when this was unsuccessful, he was unsure whether he should try to persuade Nina to seek further counselling, if not to think about separating. It was difficult to accept that although he could remain in touch with the family and even suggest possibilities for a way forward, he was powerless to change anything. Although he did manage to maintain a relationship with both Robert and Nina, there was no recognizable change or outcome.

Addressing the mind-set of the victim

In order to change a violent pattern of relationship professional help is often needed, but a pastor can sometimes play a valuable role in supporting and enabling, and being prepared to discuss the spiritual implications of what is happening in a way that most professional psychologists are not free to do. In order to be able to do this, it is of course important to reflect on your own attitudes and feelings.

People become used to mental and/or physical abuse, and often develop ways of thinking that make it hard to break out of the pattern, such as:

- This is happening to me because I deserve it.
- This is how I understand love (negative attention is better than neglect).
- I need approval and will do anything to get it.

These ways of thinking arise from a person's story and the messages they received about themselves and about the roles of men and women as they grew up. In spiritual terms they may well have an image of God that is judgemental and punitive and find it hard to accept that one might be a sinner and still be loved.

If things do change for the better in the relationship, this involves undoing deeply ingrained patterns of feeling and behaviour. Again, in a spiritual context it may be worth exploring what the meaning of suffering is in the Christian story.

If the relationship comes to an end, this involves mourning just as with any other relationship. There are losses:

- losing familiarity – the old sense of self, and the relationship,
- mourning for the relationship there might have been, either with that person or with someone else,
- mourning for the life they might have had if they had known then what they know now.

At this stage the person may be questioning God: how could God let this happen to me? Do I still believe that God is there with me?

Assessing the future is also a challenging task, not least because the end of a relationship has financial implications. The welfare of children and possibly other relatives has to be considered, along with what choices are possible. Spiritually a person in this situation may struggle with what is meant by forgiveness, and what or who they trust in as they begin again alone.

In any of these stages, a good listener who does not impose his or her own views, but helps a person to find their way through their own images of God and reactions to Scripture and liturgy is invaluable.

Some consequences of the sexual abuse of children

Nowhere is the treating the other as object rather than subject more clear than in the sexual abuse of children. It is often pointed out that the word 'paedophile' is a poor use of language, since it literally means someone who loves children, *philia* being the kind of love found in friendship, the love of Christ for his disciples. Far from loving children the paedophile uses them for his or her own ends.

The sexual abuse of children is a vast subject and there is only room here to give a few pointers to some of the consequences. It is crucial, if you have not already done so, to obtain some training in what it is and how to react when it arises. There are also many excellent publications, including sections of Kate Litchfield's *Tend My Flock* on confidentiality (pp. 22–35) and sexuality (pp. 90–

102).[17] Some other texts are listed in the bibliography at the end of this book. Do not wait for a situation to arise: familiarize yourself with the child protection policy of your diocese and/or parish and know who to turn to if you have concerns or suspicions.

Unfortunately, not all pastoral encounters with sexual abuse involve recovered memory: they are here and now situations going on in the lives of children. You may even find that abuser and abused – and their families – are both in your community. Do not try to deal with the situation alone. Make sure you understand the guidelines for disclosure, and familiarize yourself with the procedures that legally have to be followed if an accusation is made.

One of the advantages of going on a training course about sexual abuse is that it also gives you the opportunity to identify and explore some of your own reactions before you have to face them in real life situations. If you are unfortunate to be part of a community where an incidence of sexual abuse is uncovered, there will be all sorts of different feelings aroused in you as well as those around you. It is well to be prepared.

Contrary to public perception, paedophiles are not just remote elderly men in bedsits. They include the adolescent boy who sexually abuses his younger sister; the attractive woman teacher who seduces her male or female pupils; the young married man with a family. . . grandparents, uncles, teachers, friends of the family, priests, youth workers and so on. Any of them may appear in your community.

In sexual abuse, boundaries are crossed that violate a child's sense of who she or he is. It is a serious business at any age, but when it afflicts children who are still developing a sense of who they are, the effects can be devastating. The abuse itself can be anything from lifting the bed covers and watching a child while they are asleep, to caressing a child beyond what feels safe or natural; displaying your own genitals and/or masturbating in front of someone; sexual fondling; any kind of rape (oral, anal, vaginal); ritualistic practices and so on.

Maya Angelou, in her memoir, *I know Why the Caged Bird Sings*, describes being raped by her mother's boyfriend at the age

---

17 Kate Litchfield, 2006, *Tend My Flock*, Norwich: Canterbury Press.

of eight as 'a matter of the needle giving because the camel can't'. [18]
In sexual abuse, the child's body gives because the mind of the
abuser cannot or will not. Boundaries are crossed, categories broken down, chaos is let loose.

For people who experience abuse and manage to tell their story,
there are three issues that crop up again and again:

- Guilt. Many survivors believe that they are to blame.
  The violation of one's sexuality brings a heavy burden of
  shame. Guilt may also be the result of internalizing the
  abuser's rationalizations: 'Look what you made me do';
  'Your body is responding so you must like it really'. The
  fact that a child responds to sexual stimulation does not
  mean that she or he wants it to happen. The body does not
  necessarily listen to the mind.
- Fear of not being believed. Often there have been attempts
  to tell the story which have been brushed aside, trivialized
  or ignored, so that the child begins to doubt his or her
  own self.
- Loss of the abuser who may be a loved friend, relative or
  parent, as well as loss of childhood, of trust and of ordinary sexual development. The realization that you were
  not protected by those who should have loved and protected you can be one of the most painful aspects, and it
  can often be hard to access anger about this.

There are many long-term psychological effects of sexual abuse.
Childline estimates that 60–80 per cent of female prostitutes and
most male prostitutes, 60–80 per cent of adolescent or young
adult suicides and up to 50 per cent of drug addicts have been
sexually abused in childhood. At the same time there are countless
people who survive and live ordinary lives – but who are haunted
by the psychological legacy of their experience, which can include
any of the following:

---

18 Maya Angelou, 1984, *I know Why the Caged Bird Sings*, London:
Virago, pp. 75–6.

- All love becomes sexualized. It is hard to understand being loved for yourself.
- A dissociation between mind and body so that you cannot experience yourself as a physical being; the body feels dead.
- Flashbacks, panic attacks, nightmares.
- Sexual problems such as fear of penetration, fear of pregnancy.
- Symbolic physical symptoms such as mouth ulcers, womb and anal disorders.
- Difficulty in recognizing or expressing your own feelings (having been told by the abuser what your feelings should be – or having had what has happened to you trivialized by parental figures).
- Irrational fears; insomnia.
- Denial, repression, rationalization.
- Isolation, dependency, compulsive care giving.
- Inner vows ('I hate men'; 'I will never have children', etc.), whose origin may or may not be understood by the person who makes them.
- Being easily exploited and drawn into abusive relationships.
- Becoming an abuser oneself or being unable to protect one's own children – though there are many survivors who make excellent parents and are able to give their own and other children a security they never had themselves.
- Depression and deadness of feeling.
- Suicidal thoughts.
- Problems in expressing – or controlling – anger.

One of the most frequent ways children deal with sexual abuse is to forget it. It is very common for the experience to be deeply buried – repressed in the unconscious – only surfacing when some trigger brings it into consciousness. This can happen in prayer, in silence, on a retreat, in a sudden encounter with a person, or a sound or smell that is associated with the original experience. For example, one woman's journey into recovering memory of being repeatedly abused by her older step-brother began when she had a panic attack on holiday. The wallpaper of the room where they were staying was identical with the wallpaper in her childhood bedroom. For others, it might be a ticking clock, a smell of tobacco smoke, the jangling of bangles – anything that triggers an association. The fact that a person cannot remember any details does not mean it did not happen. A clock ticking and a sense of dread is a memory in itself.

When telling stories of childhood hurt and abuses people have different ways of avoiding the pain – turning humorous, turning clinical, turning matter of fact. For the story to be told as it needs to be told requires sympathetic and affirmative listening. One of the greatest fears is of not being believed. All too often parents or caregivers shy away from disclosures because they are too threatening: the idea that this might be going on in my family, my church, my workplace is unbearable. A child who tries to tell about something that is happening to him or her may be told not to be silly or not to 'talk dirty' – or even punished.

In helping the story to be told as it needs to be told it is important to show that you take it seriously ('I think we should take time to talk about this') and allow for it to be a long process. It can take years to come to terms with an abusive experience. Sometimes a person needs to tell the story many times over to accept that they are believed. Every time we empathize with and acknowledge the pain, we give more reality to the story, and the more that person can get in touch with their own reality:

> The truth about childhood is stored up in our body, and although we can repress it, we can never alter it. Our intellect can be deceived, our feelings manipulated, our perceptions confused, and our body tricked with medication. But someday the body will present its bill.[19]

One of the most painful aspects of many of these stories is the failure of protection: the mother who knew very well her

---

19 Alice Miller, 1998, *Thou Shalt Not Be Aware: Society's Betrayal of the Child*, translated from the German by H. and H. Hannum, New York: Farrar, Straus and Giroux, p. 315.

brother-in-law was going into her son's bedroom at night; the father who could not face the idea that his daughter may have been raped by his best friend. It may be essential, for a time at least, to break contact with the family of origin, especially where they refuse to accept what has happened or belittle it. Even where the family are supportive when told of the abuse, they may be unable to cope with talking about the feelings they have.

Over time it is important that the victim becomes a survivor – takes hold of their own capacity to come through the experience. Do not urge a person who has suffered abuse to forgive. This can get in the way of the healing process, and the most helpful thing you can do is reassure him or her that this can wait – the important thing for now is to recover. In a church context, it is important to be sensitive to how the word 'Father' as applied to priests or to God may affect someone who has been abused or who has not been protected by their own father. Do not insist that they use this language.

Also, some people find it easier to write down what they are feeling rather than talk about it face to face: accept this, let them know that you have read what they have written, and leave it to them to decide whether they want to talk about it as well.

In due course, for a fuller healing to take place, even the survivor identity has to be let go, though this may be years down the line, and at stressful times, the survivor identity may need to be rekindled.

Every case is different, and nowhere else in pastoral ministry is Carl Rogers' maxim, 'It is the client who knows what hurts' more relevant.[20] The aspects of the story that most appal you may not be those that are most upsetting for the person who has confided in you. If an incident seems minor to you, remember that there are many factors involved: the age of the child, the family context, threats that are made by the abuser. Remember that all sexual abuse is a serious, traumatic event that affects the whole family, and can have widespread effects in the community in which it occurs.

---

20 C. Rogers, 1961, *On Becoming a Person*, New York: Houghton Mifflin, pp. 11–12.

7

Loss (1):
'The Art of Losing'

The art of losing isn't hard to master.

Elizabeth Bishop[1]

Our third major theme is loss. In this chapter, we will consider loss generally as a part of life and also of the Christian story. There are different levels of loss: some are overcome quickly; others require the work of mourning; yet others are overwhelming. The following chapter will be devoted to factors that bring a loss into this last category. Taking death as the central example of loss, we will outline here the mourning process and the kind of support people might need at different times. In general, the Church is very good at death – but it is less good at ongoing support and at other forms of loss, particularly endings in relationships. It is worth remembering, therefore, that while we take death as the paradigm case, many of the same processes of grieving are involved in other losses.

Loss as part of life

Loss – and response to loss – runs through the Christian story. At the very beginning of the Bible, we read of the loss of Paradise and with it a whole relationship to God and creation. The incarnation brings in its wake the brutal murder of children, fulfilling the prophecy of Jeremiah: 'Rachel weeping for her children . . . because they are no more' (Matt. 2.18). To preserve Jesus's life Joseph and Mary themselves have to give up their home and escape to Egypt. Jesus's ministry culminates in his death and with it loss of hope in him as Messiah: the disciples hide away because they

---

1 The first line of 'One Art', from Elizabeth Bishop, *The Complete Poems 1927–1979*, published 1983 by Farrar, Straus & Giroux, Inc.

are afraid. Even the Resurrection does not undo the loss of Jesus. It transforms his death into a message of hope, but it does not return things to where they were. His first words to Mary Magdalene are 'Do not hold on to me' (John 20.17). Although the disciples are once more able to speak with and touch and even eat with him, he is changed and his physical presence is only temporary. He has to ascend to the Father, leaving them to teach others what he has taught them.

All these stories point to a basic fact of human existence: that loss is a universal human experience. There is a Buddhist story of a woman who went to the Buddha holding her dead son in her arms and asked him to heal him. He sent her to find a few grains of mustard seed – but, he said, they must come from a house untouched by death: neither parent nor child, servant nor animal. After a long search the woman returned, having discovered that no such house existed. She then arranged for the cremation of her son's body. It is a grim story, but the point is that though we protest – and rightly so – against death, we share it with every living creature. Whatever we have in terms of relationships, success, life satisfaction, health, prosperity – even life itself, is a temporary possession. It is not easy to take on board the simple fact noted by Maximus the Confessor that our very being is on loan to us.[2]

The Gospel stories also point to theological resources we have for dealing with loss. They tell us that loss is part of our education as children of God, learning to let go in the trust that something more will be given. Ultimately, 'those who want to save their life will lose it, and those who lose their life for my sake will save it' (Luke 9.24). There is nowhere any suggestion that loss itself is not significant. Jesus wept over the death of Lazarus even as he prepared to raise him from the dead (John 11.35). Yet, the message is repeated in different ways over and over again: for all the sorrow and trauma associated with loss it also carries the potential for transformation.

---

2 'A person is humble when he knows that his very being is on loan to him.' Maximus the Confessor, 'On the Lord's Prayer', in G. Palmer, P. Sherrard and K. Ware (trans.), 1983, *The Philokalia*, Vol. 2, London: Faber & Faber, p. 297.

The 'art of losing' is not just about endurance, but is potentially a path through sorrow to a deepening of our relationship with God. Jesus prepares the disciples for his own death by saying to them, 'Unless I leave you the Comforter cannot come' (John 16.7). His final parting in the ascension is different from that of his death on the cross. Then they were confused and abandoned. Now he says to them: 'I am with you always, to the end of the age' (Matt. 28.20). Nothing can now separate them from him. Only by finding our way through death can we come to new life: 'Unless a grain of wheat falls into the earth and dies it remains just a single grain, but if it dies, it bears much fruit' (John 12.24). The cycle of birth, death, resurrection runs through the whole of creation.

Loss, then, is unavoidable. It pervades even the most straightforward and untroubled life. In order to grow up, we have to be prepared to lose our status as children, and our parents have to be prepared to let us go. Weaning is a powerful metaphor for the loss involved in all our growing up. At every stage, we have to surrender dependence and intimacy in order to become more ourselves, and these losses have to be negotiated by parents and child in such a way that the relationship is not lost, as Kierkegaard so beautifully describes in his meditation on the story of Abraham and Isaac:

> When the child has grown and is to be weaned the mother virginally covers her breast so the child no more has a mother. Lucky the child that lost its mother in no other way. . .The mother too is not without sorrow. . .[3]

From the very beginning, then, we are all exposed to loss and vulnerable to it. We do not remember being babies, but we can be sure that the life of a baby – while full of new and joyful experiences – involves a steady process of letting go of being the centre of the universe. How that process is handled by the people caring

---

3 S. Kierkegaard, 1945, *Fear and Trembling*, trans. Alastair Hannay, London: Penguin, pp. 46–7.

for us in those very early times feeds into how we respond to loss throughout our lives.

As adults, when we enter into a relationship, follow a career or have children, we give up varying measures of autonomy and freedom. Eventually those children leave home, or there is the realization, perhaps, that one will never have children. There are losses that come from external sources: accident, illness, redundancy, theft and so on. Then come the losses of ageing – deterioration in sight, hearing, mental capacity, physical energy, and then, perhaps, the first illness or disability from which one will not recover, bringing loss of independence. Sooner or later, of course, everyone encounters the ultimate loss that is death – of parents, friends, family, partners, spouses, even children – and finally the loss that is one's own death.

Any experience of loss is a mixture of the event itself and our own way of responding to it. In *Tend My Flock*, Kate Lichfield gives a thorough and invaluable account of the ways in which loss enters into ministerial training and ministry itself, which every pastor should read.[4] Meanwhile, it is worth noticing how your original family dealt with loss so that you can identify what you may have picked up as ways of responding, and whether your own responses are similar or different – or indeed whether you want them to be!

Annie, a woman in her seventies, was referred by her GP for bereavement counselling, because her daughter had died of cancer two years before, and even allowing for the dreadfulness of the event, she appeared to be stuck in her grief. One day, she revealed that her mother had died 'of a broken heart' after Annie's brother had been killed in a car crash. After talking about what happened to her mother, she was able to say that she was not the same as her mother, and however keenly she felt her own daughter's death, she did not want to die as a result. After that, she began to be able to talk more freely about her feelings and work through her grief.

It is worth thinking, then, about losses in your own family and how they were handled: not just deaths but more ordinary losses too. How did your parents react to you starting school? becoming

---

4 Kate Litchfield, 2006, *Tend My Flock: Sustaining Good Practice in Pastoral Care*, Ch. 6.

a teenager? leaving home? Did they talk about people who died? Were children allowed at funerals? Was it OK to cry? Were there any pets who died, and if so how was it handled?

Compared with human death that of pets may seem trivial, but the death of a pet in childhood or adolescence often plays a huge part in a person's emotional life. Animals provide an experience of uncritical love and companionship that no human can. Laura, an only child, had a lop-eared pet rabbit called Droopy. She loved sitting with Droopy on her lap and stroking his ears. One summer, she went to stay with cousins for a longish holiday, and after she came back she found that sitting and stroking Droopy never felt quite the same. Only years later, as an adult, did she discover that while she was away, Droopy had died. Her parents, thinking she would be upset, had gone to some lengths to find an identical rabbit and said nothing to her. When she did find out what had happened, Laura was devastated – and it also finally made sense of that strange experience she had when Droopy did not feel quite like Droopy. In shielding her from the truth, her parents may have had the best of intentions, but they had betrayed her. She felt that in the time with the substitute rabbit she had been living under false pretences: she had not been able to mourn Droopy, nor did she have the opportunity to develop affection for a new rabbit, because all she experienced was a kind of unease.

As we go through life, we build all sorts of external and internal structures that enable us to survive and live creatively. Any major loss – a death, a redundancy, an accident that leaves you disabled – rocks that structure and may threaten to overwhelm it. It may also trigger previous losses that have not been mourned, and if a person's grief seems disproportionate, it is sometimes worth asking what other major losses there have been. It may provide clues to how they understand loss, and to unresolved losses from earlier times. It may also help to remind them of personal strengths that enabled them to survive other losses.

An understanding of loss also helps us to care for people in many different kinds of situations where loss is likely to be a key factor in what is going on: in depression or anxiety states for example or in helping people come to terms with memories of abuse. Mental, physical, sexual abuse can all deprive us of a particular relationship to our bodies, of ways of growing up or relating to others that people generally take for granted. If the situation you are dealing with seems more than you can handle, you are unlikely to go wrong if you provide support on the basis that loss is at the heart of the problem.

Bearing in mind that loss comes in many different guises, we will take death as the paradigm case and explore some of the things that happen when a person is faced with the death of someone close to them. There is a vast literature on this, so we will concentrate on those aspects that are particularly relevant to the pastoral role.

Grieving as a process

There is a considerable body of literature on stages of grief. Some people do not like the idea of stages, because they feel it puts something very personal and particular into a straitjacket. In one sense, they are right. At the beginning of *Hamlet*, the king complains of Hamlet's excessive grief for his dead father, while his mother reminds him that death happens all the time: 'Thou know'st 'tis common, all that lives must die, Passing through nature to eternity.' Hamlet points out that nevertheless his grief is particular: ''Tis not . The forms, moods, shows of grief that can denote me truly. . .I have within, which passeth show; These but the trappings and the suits of woe.'[5]

Nevertheless, there is a general pattern to grief, though it is as well to remember that it is not rigid. People may find themselves moving forward and backward through the various processes or in and out of different states. An anniversary, for example, a whiff of spring or a visit to a place that was important in the relationship – or indeed another bereavement – may trigger a fresh experience of grief even after a long time.

Broadly there are four main phases of grief that are commonly experienced:

- shock and disbelief,
- experiencing the loss,

---

5 *Hamlet*, Act I scene 2.

- disorientation,
- rebuilding.

Shock and disbelief

The first reaction to a major loss is usually to go into a state of shock. Something unmanageable has happened and body and mind combine to protect you from it. The same thing often happens with a physical injury. One evening, I slipped and broke a bone my foot and walked several hundred yards home and went to bed. It was only in the early hours of the morning that the pain set in, and I realized there was no way I could put my foot to the ground. People have different ways of being in shock. C. S. Lewis described it as being like a physical anxiety ('I never knew grief felt so like fear');[6] some people are inclined to retreat inside themselves, becoming a blank wall; others may be unable to stop talking, or chain smoking, or fidgeting. After a death there is usually a lot to be done, and a still, calm, competent presence of someone who can liaise with the outside world, see to children, answer the phone, feed the cat and make cups of tea – who can be on hand if wanted and invisible if not – is invaluable.

Most people experience periods of disbelief in early bereavement, and this can operate on different time scales depending on the nature of the relationship. The loss becomes most obvious when the dead person is not where one expects them to be. If the person who died lived in the same house, the loss will be constantly re-experienced every time they are not at breakfast or do not come home in the evening. If, on the other hand, the dead person is someone you only see once or twice a month, the sense of disbelief may recur over quite a long period of time, whenever you find they are not where you expected them to be.

Between the death and the funeral, people often experience a kind of limbo. With a funeral comes ritual, a sharing of the loss with the wider community and sometimes emotional catharsis. At the same time, the evening after the funeral is often particularly difficult. It is

---

6 The opening sentence of C. S. Lewis, 1961, *A Grief Observed*, London: Faber and Faber, p. 7.

always worth checking where the bereaved person will be after every-one has gone home and whether they want someone with them.

The value of ritual in grief is also worth remembering with losses that are less obvious than death. Diane, for example, had never married or had a family, and as she approached her sixtieth birthday she realized that many of her friends were celebrating silver or ruby weddings and the birth or baptisms of grandchildren. This made her feel extremely lonely. She understood that her friends, too, were growing older, but that their ceremonies of anniversaries and new life helped to ease the process. What rites of passage were there for a single person? She talked with her parish priest and together they devised a service based on a num-ber of psalms and readings that expressed something of what she felt about this landmark. It was held close to Diane's sixtieth birthday with a number of friends taking part. She went on to take the opportunity to contact a number of old friends with whom contact had lapsed, and this too helped her reframe her history and move on.

Experiencing the loss

The funeral, of course, is only the beginning. Once it is over, there is often a general expectation that everything will be back to nor-mal. Ruth was a vicar's wife, whose husband died after 40 years of marriage. Two months after he died she was greeted by a fellow parishioner outside the church who said, 'I expect you are over your little trouble now.' For a person who is grieving, however, the process is only just beginning. He or she is learning to live with absence where there was previously a significant presence – in the house, at work, at school, at the pub, on walking holidays. At all these times, there is the lack of particular conversation, companionship or sense of humour. This may also be a time when a person realizes that the chance to heal a damaged relationship with a parent, a child, a friend, has now been lost, and grief can involve guilt and anger as well as sorrow.

During this period, your capacity as a pastor to tolerate pain – simply to be able to be there with the feelings without wanting to tidy anything up – will be invaluable. Intense grief is like a raw wound: even exposure to the air can irritate and hurt it, yet may also be part of the healing. For this reason, the presence of other people can quickly become overwhelming – as can the loneliness when no one is around. You cannot fill the loneliness, but a regular contact – a phone call or a visit – can provide a framework that helps in some small way towards containing it.

Disorientation

If the first task of grieving is to take in the fact of the loss, the second is to experience the pain. The initial, acute pain is often followed by a sense of disorientation. The change brought about by the death may be so great that it can threaten a person's very sense of self. Melanie Klein (1882–1960) was one of the first to develop Freud's thinking about mourning and melancholia and to bring loss to the forefront of psychoanalytic thinking. She likened it to an early state in infancy, when as babies we had to begin to make sense of ourselves as separate beings and to relate to the world as other than ourselves.[7] This can involve feelings of:

- Anxiety – I'm all alone and I don't know who I am.
- Guilt – Have I destroyed the people I love by not realizing that they had needs too?
- Paranoia – If the world is separate from me, how do I know if it cares for me or will attack me?
- Despair – I was comfortable and happy where I was and don't want to lose it.

We will explore these in some detail.

Anxiety

Anxiety may be unconscious but expressed through the body. As Lewis describes it: 'I am not afraid, but the sensation is like being afraid. The same fluttering in the stomach, the same restlessness,

---

7 M. Klein, 1940, 'Mourning and Its Relation to Manic Depressive States', in Juliet Mitchell (ed.), 1986, *The Selected Melanie Klein*, London: Hogarth Press, pp. 146–74.

the yawning. I keep on swallowing.'[8] In acute bereavement, people are accident prone, and their immunity is low.

For some people, a significant aspect of grieving is to become frighteningly aware of one's own mortality. It may be that a sudden accident had made a person aware of how things can change in a moment: 'This time last year we had no idea he could just be wiped out like that.' Or there may have been a long and distressing confrontation with illness leading to a preoccupation with health: 'Am I going to die the same way?'

Where there was an illness, it is quite common to develop the symptoms the dead person had – high blood pressure, digestive problems or whatever. Often there is no underlying cause, and the symptoms pass, but perhaps they show how closely we may identify with the person who has died. Similarly, people whose parents died young often develop symptoms the dead parent had, when they approach the age at which the parent died. They may start taking out life insurance policies they can't afford, or be constantly at the doctor's – or never at the doctor's for fear of what they might find out. It is always important to check out whether there is a physical problem, but such symptoms can often indicate an underlying anxiety that they too will die young.

The work of an American existentialist therapist, Irvin D. Yalom, suggests that there is a negative correlation between life satisfaction and death anxiety.[9] Similarly Averil Stedeford's research at Sobell House hospice in Oxford suggests that unresolved problems in areas such as work, family and relationships can increase depression and anxiety during the process of dying, and that the opportunity to work through them enables a more peaceful death.[10]

Death anxiety can take a more complicated form where what is at stake is psychological rather than physical survival: 'I don't know what I shall do without him/her.' 'I feel as though part of myself is missing.' If the anxiety is excessive it can prove impossible

---

8 C. S. Lewis, *Grief*, p. 7.

9 I. D. Yalom, 1980, *Existential Psychotherapy*, New York: Basic Books, Ch. 4.

10 A. Stedeford, 1984, *Facing Death*, London: Heinemann Medical Books, Ch. 10.

to come to terms with one's own mortality: either the inevitability of death, or anxiety about one's ability to survive without the lost person or thing.

Another common anxiety symptom is agoraphobia – literally fear of the marketplace – being frightened to go out. Here, a companion on the way, someone who can reliably befriend the person and mediate the outside world, can enable recovery without professional treatment.

A different way of being anxious is the 'grandiose' solution: carrying on as though nothing has happened and never allowing anything to be different. In this situation, the dead person may be used as a weapon: 'Your father wouldn't like you to do that, dear'; 'If your mother were alive you would never speak to me like that.' Everything has to be as it was and no new relationship can develop, with family or with old friends or new.

These are all useful and necessary mechanisms, but if there is to be any moving on, then sooner or later they need to give way to an honest confrontation with loss.

Guilt

Losing a person or a loved object makes us angry, and this all too easily gets turned against oneself in guilt. 'If only I'd got him to the doctor sooner.' 'I can't stop thinking about the day she wanted me to go to the garden centre and I was too busy – was I always too busy?' 'So-and-so would not have wanted me to feel like this.' 'I should be doing something constructive instead of moping around.' Some of this kind of questioning is natural, and indeed part of the process of coming to terms with the past, but it can become obsessional, particularly where the relationship has been difficult. In a similar way, someone who has lost a job or had a bad accident may get so stuck in worrying about what they did wrong that it is hard to move on.

Paranoia

In a state of loss, the world becomes an unfriendly place: contact with it is a constant reminder of what has been lost. If this takes hold a person may refuse all offers of help or support, and avoid all new possibilities for fear of getting hurt again. Patience is required to coax them back into relationship.

Despair

Despair is different from sadness. Sadness lives; despair dies. People who have experienced depression know that there is a deadness about them in depression that is not there in sadness. Sadness may be acute and painful, but it is not dead.

Questioning faith

Bereavement often brings a crisis in faith. A person who has been very confident in what they believe may be profoundly rocked and need help in coming to terms with a different relationship to the God they thought they loved and trusted. In *A Grief Observed*, C. S. Lewis faces the reality of pain and torment in a way that for him is entirely new. It is not unusual to want no more to do with a God who allows the world to be like this. Other people may find that grief puts them in touch with the numinous: what was merely a form of words before acquires a new ring of truth. Many people also begin to think for the first time about what they actually do believe, and what the words of the Creed and the prayers mean – because they really need to know.

As a pastor, you cannot expect to have all the answers, but if you can find the courage to hear the same questions in yourself – to be in touch with parts of yourself that do not believe, that are disillusioned, that maybe even sometimes hate God – you will not be afraid to hear them from other people. Reflect on what really speaks to you personally in Scripture and in liturgy about the meaning of death and resurrection. Bear in mind also that a shared silence can be more valuable than saying too much. You do have powerful theological resources at your disposal, but they need to be applied with great care and personal authenticity if they are not to do more harm than good.

Anger, guilt and anxiety form a powerful cocktail with sadness. For some people, faith can become another stick to beat themselves with: 'I should not feel like this because she has gone to a better place.' As a pastor who senses that anxiety is playing a large part in a person's grief it is important not to be too quick to reassure, but rather to encourage reality testing, and to get talking about the events that led to the death, and acknowledge their power. Only then may it be possible to help the person to build hope for their own future.

Rebuilding

In a major bereavement, it can be a relief to find one has somehow come through the first year, but the second year can bring with it a harsh realism that was previously softened by the closeness of the memories. By now most people will have completed all the practical tasks associated with the death: there is a new life to be lived that does not include the dead person.

Eventually most people will begin to pick up the threads of a new life. It does not happen overnight, and there may be many false starts. Sometimes the thought that this might mean one has ceased to care about or remember the dead person can be a real blockage, and the Church's practice of special prayers or services on anniversaries can be very helpful here, marking stages on the journey for both the living and the dead.

Two things are needed psychologically in order to move on, to master the 'art of losing'. One is to be able to let go of the past, and the other is to have 'internalized' what has been lost so that it remains part of your life. In simple terms, this means that if a person has lost someone who loved and affirmed them, they can now find that love and affirmation within, even though that person is no longer there.

This accounts for the mysterious fact that it can be in some ways easier to mourn a good relationship than one that has been neglectful, hostile or ambivalent, because the good relationship has given its gift: 'the better part which will not be taken away' (Luke 10.42). We become who we are through our relationships, and it is through nourishing relationships that we build up a sense of self that is resilient to loss.

Our lives are full of meetings and partings, separations, endings. These are cause for conflicting emotions: sadness, anger, excitement, relief and often all of these things together. Finding a way through these can be hard, and the Church has a great resource in liturgy and ritual. Through these it provides a holy space, a healing space, which can hold together things that grief prefers to drive apart. As a pastor you have the experience of such spaces through the Church, and also the opportunity to create them by developing your tolerance of conflicting emotions, learning to sit with them and allow prayer to do its work, whether in your own life or someone else's.

Summary – toolkit

Remember that loss is a part of everyone's life. Even if you yourself have not experienced the death of someone close to you, you do have experiences of loss to draw on.

The stages or states of mourning are better seen as overlapping and cyclical than as a linear progression. They can be divided into four clusters:

- shock, disbelief,
- realizing the pain of the loss,
- disorientation, yearning, anger, anxiety and guilt,
- reorganization, recovery, reinvestment.

While bereavement through death is the paradigm case, the same things may have to be lived through in other forms of loss such as redundancy, loss of a home, physical disability, children leaving home and so on.

Some grief reactions

- anxiety, agoraphobia, restlessness, fear of own death,
- anger and guilt,
- searching: trying to find the lost person or thing in some other form; rushing into replacement relationships,
- identification: developing symptoms experienced by the person who died,
- loss of sense of self, leading to despair, apathy, suicidal thoughts,
- crisis in religious faith: questioning, rejection or a new interest,
- a general shut down of emotions.

Some do's and don'ts:

DO

- give time;
- encourage talking about the loss, about good times and bad (what is missed and what it is a relief to miss);
- allow tears;
- accept anger;
- tolerate uncertainty;
- explain the normality of the process without minimizing it;
- arrange practical support where needed.

DON'T

- give advice;
- try to cheer up;
- minimize the loss;
- try to solve the problem.

8

Loss (2):
When Grief is Overwhelming

Why are some people overwhelmed by grief?

The capacity to accommodate loss – to mourn – is not built in to human beings: it is learned through a lifetime of experiencing loss. It is also fundamental to mental health. Any mourning process involves a relationship between the inner and outer resources of the bereaved person and the nature of the loss itself. At the same time, some losses are undoubtedly more difficult to absorb than others, and some defy any attempt to make sense of them: 'This can't be unravelled, it can only be wept through.'[1]

Again taking death as the paradigm case, in this chapter we will look at ways in which the mind avoids the pain of mourning and some of the consequences of that. We will also outline some danger signals to look out for and guidelines for coming alongside unprocessed loss.

Denial: avoiding the pain of mourning

Denial is a difficult word because it seems to suggest that someone chooses to deny something that is obvious. When it is used as a technical term in psychology, however, it refers to a protective unconscious process that prevents the truth getting through, not a conscious choice. Where death is concerned, it can operate in different ways.

---

1 A statement by a psychotherapy patient quoted in Murray Cox, 1988, *Structuring the Therapeutic Process: Compromise with Chaos*, London: Jessica Kingsley.

At one extreme, there is behaving as though the death had never happened. In Dickens' novel, *Great Expectations*, Miss Havisham is a wealthy spinster, who falls in love with a man who actually only wants to swindle her out of her inheritance. While she is dressing for their wedding, she receives a letter from him: he has taken her money and deserted her. She has all the clocks stopped at the exact time – 20 minutes to 9 – that she received his letter and stays in her decaying mansion, never removing her wedding dress and leaving the wedding cake uneaten on the table.

At the other end of the spectrum is the person who removes anything that serves as a reminder that the dead person ever existed. This is a common reaction in adolescence after the break-up of a relationship: any letters, cards, gifts are destroyed; clothes that were bought for special outings or holidays are given away; music that was shared is never listened to again. The other person is cleared away as though they had never been.

While it is possible to carry on after a death as though nothing has happened, this is usually at a cost. Oliver's father died suddenly when Oliver was 15, and while his mother and sisters dissolved into grief, he became strong, silent and practical. He was now the man of the family. Things might have developed differently if it had not been for an incident at school. One day when he suddenly felt tearful during a maths lesson, the maths master eyed him sternly and said, 'We all have problems, Oliver.' From this he understood that school was not an appropriate place to bring his feelings either. He went on to do spectacularly well in his O and A levels, but did not take up a place at university. Instead, he apprenticed himself to a plumber near home so that he could continue to be around to support his mother. Eventually he set up his own business in which he worked extremely hard and married his secretary. He was bewildered when his wife left him for another man – a man, she said, who was willing to listen to her feelings. Oliver did not believe in feelings. The strength that had attracted his wife to him in the first place turned out to be too brittle to sustain an intimate relationship with her.

When you suspect something like this may be happening, the kindest thing you can do probably is to encourage the person concerned to slow down and make space for the pain to emerge, at whatever age. Jane, whose mother died when she was 12, had a very different school experience from Oliver. One of her most healing memories from that time was when she felt bad, she was allowed to go to the school nurse who used to let her curl up in sick bay under a duvet until she felt able to go back into class.

Where denial has taken hold, however, we can find that grief is

* delayed,
* masked,
* chronic.

Delayed grief

In delayed grief, the mourning process has been inhibited or post-poned at the time of the loss. Then, months or even years later, something apparently trivial triggers a major reaction. For example, Stacey appeared inordinately upset after she lost a bracelet while swimming in the sea. She herself did not understand why. It later emerged that the previous year she had suffered a miscar-riage. At the time, she had brushed it off as unimportant, but this new lesser incident where something she treasured had slipped away from her triggered all the grief she had not felt at the time.

As with Oliver, one reason for delayed grief is that at the time of the original loss there were other crises, or people to look after. Lizzie's husband had a sudden heart attack the summer that her daughter, Felicity, was about to take her A levels. Lizzie felt that it would be terrible for Felicity's career to suffer because of her father's sudden death, and as soon as the funeral was over she devoted all her energy to supporting her through her exams. Felicity did well and won a place at university for that autumn. During the summer, Lizzie encouraged Felicity to talk about her grief with friends and family and to seek the support of the college counsel-lor, when she arrived at university.

As far as she herself was concerned, she deliberately postponed her own grieving until after Felicity had gone, thinking there would be plenty of opportunity to let go then, hardly realizing that she now faced the double loss of her husband's death and her daughter leaving home. Almost immediately, however, her brother became ill with cancer, and when he died Lizzie was completely taken up with supporting her widowed mother. Her mother never recovered from her son's death and died two years later. By now, Lizzie was so used to caring for everyone else that she had more or less forgotten her own feelings. She picked up her career as a nurse and involved herself in church life, where she was a valued member of the pastoral team.

After several years, the time came for her to retire, and it was then that she found herself overwhelmed by a cocktail of sadness, anxiety and anger. She found herself deeply envious of her friends, who had living partners or spouses, and gradually she realized that she resented her husband for dying, and she resented being alone with no one alongside her in old age. She was able to work through these feelings with a counsellor. Towards the end of that work, she arranged a memorial service for her husband, her brother and her mother and this provided a ritual space in which she experienced her grief as held in the wider community. She remained closely involved with the church, but now she had learned to accept support as well as to give it.

Masked grief

Masked grief is when a person is not aware of their grief but it emerges in psychosomatic symptoms or difficult behaviour. Stealing in particular can be an attempt to compensate for loss, and this is particularly common in children, where stealing, disruptive behaviour, aggression and so on often have loss at their root.

This may include losses such as moving house, the arrival of a new sibling, the death of a grandparent, the disappearance of one or other parent after a separation. To understand the loss for what it is, rather than focusing on the behavioural symptom, may hold the seeds of change, as in the film, *The Kid with a Bike*,[2] a moving fictional account of a ten-year-old boy who is desperate after his father has left him. Ten-year-old Cyril is in care and refuses all evidence that his father has really abandoned him. He meets Samantha, a hairdresser, who begins to foster him at weekends,

---

2 Dardenne Brothers, 2011.

and their relationship is sorely tested when he becomes involved with a local drug dealer. Through sticking with unconditional love that nevertheless sets boundaries to what she will accept, she does in the end enable him to begin to come to terms with his situation.

Chronic and exaggerated grief

In chronic grief, everyone gets tired of the stuck record. 'I never look forward to anything since Harry had his heart attack' – but Harry's heart attack happened 30 years ago. In exaggerated grief, anxiety becomes phobia, guilt becomes suicidal, sadness becomes depression, and for those around there can be an overwhelming sense of helplessness. Often the dead person is idealized so that no one else can possibly match up to him or her, and not a word can be said against them. Chronic grief often slips into long-term depression and can be hard to distinguish from it. It may be helpful if you can probe the reality: 'What don't you miss?' The answer might be anything – the snoring, the fussing in the kitchen, the never doing the washing up, for example.

Suicidal thoughts

Depression may at first be protective, because it deadens the feelings, but if it persists for a long time it can lead to despair, hopelessness and even suicide.

If someone hints at suicidal thoughts, never be afraid to talk about it with them – why they are thinking of killing themselves, how they imagine doing it. Who would be affected, and how? It may be because they cannot see a future or cannot bear the pain. It may be a way of getting back at other people who are experienced as neglectful. It may be because they want to be with a person who has died. It is particularly important to explore their beliefs about the afterlife – and be prepared to look at your own.

If you are aware that someone is a suicide risk, ask their permission to contact their GP, or persuade them to tell their doctor themselves. If they have a lot of painkillers in the house, try to persuade them to store the pills with a trusted friend or neighbour rather than keep the means of an overdose at hand.

Bereavement by suicide is, of course, particularly devastating as well as isolating. A regular space to talk without being judged or told not to dwell on the events can be invaluable.

Some risk factors to look out for after a loss

The way a loss happens can powerfully affect the ability to come to terms with it, and this applies to losses such as illness and disability as well as bereavement through death.

Some factors that increase the risk of having difficulty in coming to terms with a death are:

- traumatic circumstances, such as an accident or violence,
- some other life crisis going on at the same time,
- a highly ambivalent close relationship with the dead person,
- a poor support network.

When planning a funeral visit or visiting a bereaved person, it is well to be aware that the nature of the death itself can have a profound effect on their state of mind:

- Was the death sudden, or did it follow a period of preparation?
- Was it by illness or an accident?
- Who found the dead person? Where was the bereaved person at the time of death?
- If there was an illness how did the dead person deal with it (denial, courage, anger, depression, relief)? Were they able to talk about it?
- Was it a timely death after a long and fulfilled life, or that of a young person, a child or a baby? Was it a stillbirth?
- Is there anyone to blame? – doctors, drivers, relatives, drug dealers . . .
- Was it carried out by someone else – murder or manslaughter?
- Was it suicide? (This brings with it very special problems –

see Further Reading at the end of this book for some suggested reading.)

- Is there a body? Was it seen? Was it mutilated? If there is
no body (e.g. after a death at sea), are we sure there is a
death?
- Where did the death take place? While many people – and
those caring for them – are grateful for the opportunity to
die at home, it is worth being aware that if the hospital (in
the form of equipment) has come to the home, rather than
the patient to the hospital, the relatives cannot walk away
from it when the person dies. Although beds, hoists and so
on can be delivered almost straight away when needed, the
suppliers do not expect to collect them from your home
for up to two weeks after the death, and their presence can
be very distressing.

Some general factors that are likely to affect the way a person
comes through the mourning process are:

- the nature of the relationship,
- the developmental stage of the bereaved person,
- the social network.

The nature of the relationship

A crucial factor in mourning is the nature of the relationship. Was
it a relationship of companionship and mutuality or one of need
and exploitation? Were feelings shared and discussed? Was there
a long and gruelling period of caring? Husband, wife, parent,
child, friend, lover – all these relationships and many others have
particular relevance in death.

Particularly hard is 'disenfranchised', grief when the relationship with the dead person was for whatever reason not recognized
by the outside world, perhaps because it was never accepted or
because of a family feud – or simply because nobody except the
two people involved understood how close it was.

Death does not wait around for a convenient moment and can
crash in on some other crisis that is going on in a person's work

or home life. It is worth remembering this, and making space to talk about other concerns when appropriate.

The developmental stage of the bereaved person

The developmental stage of a bereaved person does not necessarily match their chronological age. Married couples, for example, often divide up the tasks of living, so that perhaps the wife has never grappled with bills, council tax, mortgage payments and so on, while the husband has never really lived alone in his own home or prepared a meal for himself. They may feel helpless in these areas.

As we have seen, a loss can trigger feelings from previous losses that have not been mourned, and you may find yourself dealing with someone who seems much younger than they actually are. Children and adolescents are, of course, particularly vulnerable, and it is worth acquainting yourself with local groups specifically to help them. Fortunately, the practice of excluding children from funerals is much less prevalent than it used to be, though you may well be asked what you think about children coming to the funeral, and it is worth being prepared for this question. The most important thing is not to lie to children. They always detect it, and end up more anxious. This does not mean being brutal with the truth, but it does mean finding ways to tell it that break it gently, holding together both the reality of death and the reality of Christian hope.

When breaking bad news to anyone, but to children in particular, it is a good principle to start from where they are. A child, for example, may already have experienced a family member being ill. From there, you can move step by step to what has happened – but beware of setting up an anxiety that anyone who is ill is going to die.

The social network

Ongoing social support is a key factor in recovering from loss, and family, friends and community can all help at different levels.

As time goes on, it is always worth checking out whether a bereaved person wants a visit or to come to an event, or to be involved in a project – and to be prepared for a refusal. This does not necessarily mean they are isolating themselves: so much goes on in acute loss that the presence of other people is far more intense than usual, and people quickly become overwhelmed. If you do meet with a 'no', don't be afraid to ask if you can offer again in a week or two. Be alert to the flurry of activity around the time of the funeral and the intense loneliness that can follow when that dies down.

Deaths often open up possibilities for reconciliation in families where there have been feuds or estrangements. Be prepared to encourage these, but watch out for people getting too close too quickly, leading to further hurt.

The ongoing family life of a parish – simply to be part of something where the rhythms of birth, life and death continue and are contained – can have immense value in itself in addition to any individual support. Never be afraid to refer to the death when you meet a person going through a bereavement: they will almost always thank you for it. Find out where they are, not where you think they should be. This may sound obvious, but there is a powerful temptation to try and tidy up other people's emotions.

A particular case is clergy spouses whose husbands or wives die in full-time ministry. In addition to the death, they usually face a multiple loss. They lose not only their home, but also their parish community, since it is usual to move away from the parish to make space for the new incumbent. There may or may not be financial provision, and they may need help in sorting this out. This also, of course, applies to anyone living in tied accommodation and makes them – and any children living at home – particularly vulnerable.

When should you worry?
Just as loss is part of life, so is the mourning process, and support through the emotional and practical difficulties will help this to take place. Bearing in mind individual differences both in temperament and circumstances, it is worth watching out for some danger signals:

- Intense fresh grief whenever the dead person is mentioned. This is quite normal for the first few weeks or months, and at anniversaries, but should gradually subside over time. Generally you could expect acute grief to have given way by the end of two years, even if there is a continuing awareness of loss.
- Excessive reactions to relatively minor losses, for example being unduly upset when a distant acquaintance dies. The intensity of grief is in a strange way addictive, and while bereaved people can support each other by sharing their experiences, beware of the person who is too eager to enter into other people's grief before they are through their own. You will find that most hospices and bereavement counselling services do not accept volunteers to work with them, until they are two years away from a major bereavement. Bear this in mind if you yourself are bereaved.[3]
- Extreme reactions of the Miss Havisham kind – or their opposite.
- A history of depression.
- False euphoria.
- Self-harm or self-destructive impulses.
- Chronic anxiety and phobias.

How can you help?

Above all, allow space, and do not try to solve anything (except practical matters that are within your remit!). Remember that every bereavement is particular. You have your own experience of the landscape of loss, but only that person can tell you what it means to them. Don't be afraid simply to spend time with a person in distress. It is often all that is needed. As a bereavement counsellor in the early 1990s, I often noticed clergy referring people within the first few months after a death, when there was nothing unusual about what they were going through, as though they might be afraid of the person's grief. At the same time, do not

---

3 See Kate Litchfield, 2006, *Tend My Flock: Sustaining Good Pastoral Care*, Norwich: Canterbury Press, Ch. 6.

be afraid to ask for help from doctors, psychiatrists or counsellors, if you really feel it is needed. It may even be that you yourself find the other person's grief hard to bear and need someone to talk to.

Encourage the bereaved person to get any physical symptoms checked out, and find out any genetic implications if this is relevant. It may be easier to provide false reassurance, but it is also irresponsible.

Test the reality of the dead person and the relationship. Encourage talk about them between various people who knew them. Allow for celebration and regret. Try to avoid idealization, and don't be afraid to remember the dead person's quirks, sense of humour, idiosyncracies and bloody-mindedness. 'She could be dreadful but I loved her anyway' is much healthier than 'She was the best woman who ever lived.'

Do not be afraid to explore what the bereaved person believes happens after death. It may be different from what you believe, and you need to be prepared to let that be, even if you share what you yourself believe.

In a pastoral context, prayer for the dead is also an important issue. In some Christian traditions it is central; in others it is forbidden and everything has to be handed over to God. You yourself may have difficulty with one practice or the other. Know what your own stance is, and be prepared to accept the other person's if it is different.

With or without prayer, many people have experiences of a dead loved person as being present with them. Some people find this comforting; others find it frightening and may need reassurance that it does not mean they are going mad. There is often a sense of the dead person going on a journey, and gradually getting further away.

Geraldine, whose mother died after a long illness, was deeply comforted by what she experienced as visits from her mother, a real sense of presence, and she got in the habit of making space sometimes to sit and think about her mother in a way that almost seemed to summon her up. A year or two after her mother had died, she began to feel uncomfortable with this, as though she was dragging her mother back from somewhere that she should not interfere with. Realizing this was an important part of letting go of her own grief.

Knowing yourself

In your training, you will almost certainly have been asked to think about your own experiences of loss, but they do not stop when you begin ministry. There may be times when you are in crisis or experiencing a loss or a period of doubt or disillusionment that makes it very hard for you to be present to a person who is grieving.

If at all possible, talk to someone you trust about this, and do not be afraid to ask for help in providing the necessary care. It may be that you are not the best person to take on this particular task at this time.

Much good work is done in pastoral ministry on the basis of the pastor as 'wounded healer' and this is vitally important. We do need to be aware of our own wounds in tending those of others.[4] At the same time, one of the most common causes of disaster in pastoral relationships is what is known as 'coincidence of need'. Two people who might normally be able to help and support each other come together when they are both under such emotional stress that they have no room for the other's grief.

Paddy and his sister Janet had always been close, and he supported Janet during hard months, when she nursed her dying husband and was there for her at the time of the death. He did not pay much attention to the fact that during this he was unexpectedly made redundant from the firm he had worked for for 30 years. After all, he had no financial worries, and it was nothing compared with what Janet was going through. It was only when the funeral was over that he began to find that, far from being glad of the time he had available to spend with his sister, he found her presence very upsetting and irritating. He would go home angry and pour himself a stiff drink. At the same time he felt extremely guilty about this and talked about it with his minister who suggested that perhaps

---

4 See Henry Nouwen, 1979, *The Wounded Healer: Ministry in Contemporary Society*, New York: Image and Doubleday.

he and Janet were suffering from coincidence of need: it was not that Paddy did not care for her, but his capacity to do so was badly reduced by his own loss. The minister encouraged him to seek help in coming to terms with his redundancy, and in due time he became able to be more available to his sister.

At times when you yourself are facing major loss, some self-protection may be the kindest course, not only for you but for those in your care.

Finally, most people do come through. Although two years is considered the normal limit for the acute phases of grieving, recovery is often slow, and it may be several years before there is a sea change, or a readiness for a new relationship. One of the great gifts of church life is the continuity of the yearly cycle through time, witnessing to the ongoing renewal of God's presence in creation.

PART 3

Some Specific Issues in Mental Health

9

What is Mental Health?

> The mentally healthy individual is one who faces life and copes
> with it to the best of his ability and, at the same time remembers
> that he is a member of society and respects the rights of every
> member of that society, *including himself.*
>
> *Mabel Ross*[1]

When it comes to the specifics of mental health, it helps if you have
some reference points as to the seriousness of what you encounter.
This is not always easy to judge even for professionals, and is a
constant problem for pastors: when should you go the extra mile?
When should you shake the dust from off your feet? What limits
can you or should you set? When should you seek further help?

Generally there are three types of norms for mental health:

- statistical,
- functional,
- social.

A **statistical norm** assumes that what the majority does is normal.
At a basic everyday level it may be of some use, but it is internally
illogical since frequency of a behaviour or symptom does not
imply it is healthy or otherwise. We also know that entire communities or nations can be swept up in a collective madness: the rise
of National Socialism in Germany in the 1930s is an example.

Functional norms distinguish between healthy and disturbed functioning, asking questions like 'Can this person sustain relationships?'
'Can they turn up to work on time?' 'Can they get through the day

---

1 M. Ross, 1949, 'For Today's Children and Tomorrow's Adults', *Educational Leadership*, 6:8, pp. 491–5.

without a quart of vodka?' According to Freud, healthy functioning is to be able to love and to work, which is not a bad definition provided we interpret the concept of 'work' broadly to include many different ways of being in society. Donald Winnicott added to this the importance of belonging to some kind of community:

> We need to accept that psychiatrically healthy persons depend for their health and for their personal fulfilment on loyalty to a delimited area of society, perhaps the local bowls club.[2]

In our fragmented society the churches play a huge part in providing a sense of belonging – and contributing – for people who would otherwise be isolated.

Of course, countless people with mental health problems do manage to love and to work and to belong to communities. As Winnicott says, we depend on these frameworks to maintain a degree of mental health, and it is when we lose any one of them, that we are most at risk.

Social norms define what is acceptable and may treat deviance from that as illness. Some would go so far as to say that all mental illness is arbitrarily defined by social norms. We label something as disordered because we find it unacceptable. This in turn sets up an expectation, and paradoxically can reinforce the deviant role and behaviour. This can affect both individuals and groups, as often happens, for example, with adolescents.

If we take this further, we can even argue that mental ill health is not so much disease as an understandable and sane response to a sick society. The person who exhibits the symptoms can be thought of as carrying the sickness for the rest of us, and the person who is functioning may be no more sane than the person in a psychiatric ward – just better defended against reality.[3]

---

2 D. W. Winnicott, 2005, *Playing and Reality*, London: Routledge Classics, p. 190.

3 The great proponent of this view in the 1960s was R. D. Laing (1927–89). His seminal work *The Divided Self* (London: Penguin, 1960) is still well worth reading. In contemporary psychology, too, there is an increasing understanding of some forms of mental ill-health as being connected with difficulty in filtering incoming information.

Social norms, of course, change over time. The removal of homosexuality from the American Psychiatric Association's list of psychiatric disorders in 1977 is an example – and of course there are organizations, including church-based ones, which do not accept this shift.

A spiritual dimension

Every day we are confronted with suffering, fears, fantasies, isolation and alienation. They can be hard to accept or explain, but we all share them as human beings. Every one of us has uncharted areas of psyche, pockets of madness into which we may fall at different times in our lives.

Oh the mind, mind has mountains; cliffs of fall
Frightful, sheer, no-man-fathomed. Hold them cheap
May who ne're hung there.

Gerard Manley Hopkins[4]

As Christians, we have to live with the elusiveness of God's presence as well as with the cultural anxiety that God may be dead, or never existed or was invented out of our own need, or has abandoned us. At the same time, we are daily exposed to extremes of violence, war and distress through modern media. This heightened exposure can make it hard to trust in a loving God, though this is, of course, not a new problem, Dostoevsky's Grand Inquisitor being perhaps the supreme example in literature.[5]

Contemporary spirituality has to take on board our all too obvious fragility while also building awareness of our interdependence. To be alive at all is to experience insecurity and anxiety, and anxiety is best contained by the presence of a trusted other. This 'other' may be a person, an animal, a community, a building, a reliable cycle of events – where again the liturgical cycle can play an important part. It may also be a loved person who has died or

---

4 From 'No worst, there is none', in W. H. Gardner and N. H. Mackenzie (eds), 1970, *The Poems of Gerard Manley Hopkins*, London: Penguin, p. 100.

5 See F. Dostoevsky, 1990, *The Brothers Karamazov*, trans. R. Pevear and L. Volkhonsky, London: Vintage, pp. 246ff.

gone away, but who has become part of our internal world, or even someone in history or literature who touches us and gives us courage. We may perhaps think of such a person as an adopted ancestor.

In helping others, we do need to learn to distinguish between voluntary vulnerability and availability which is a Christian path, and a victimization of oneself or others which is neurotic. We cannot give away what we do not already possess, and we all need to accept that there are people we are simply unable to help – though this does not mean that no one can help them. Being familiar with local specialized resources is an important aspect of being a pastor.

Neurosis and psychosis

When thinking about mental health it is important to remember that different psychological profiles have both their positive and negative aspects. Kevin Dutton's book, *The Wisdom of Psychopaths*, charts the similarities in psychology between the person who becomes a serial killer and the one who rises to the top in business or becomes a brilliant surgeon – or charismatic clergyperson.[6] The same applies to the healing techniques used in psychology. The abuse of psychiatric drugs in Soviet Russia is well known – but it is also the case that empathy, a vital tool in the healing work of psychotherapy, is also essential to the art of an advertising executive – or a torturer.

When we describe the following tendencies, therefore, this is not in order to encourage labelling of people in your community, but to provide ways of thinking about how people – including ourselves – tend to interact with each other. These are ways of looking at different kinds of tendency which we all have in some degree.

The first distinction that is often made in psychiatry is between neurosis and psychosis. In general, neurosis refers to the more everyday problems we all experience, but which may develop in such a way that they interfere with our functioning and require professional help. A person suffering from psychosis is more likely

---

6 Kevin Dutton, 2012, *The Wisdom of Psychopaths*, London: Heinemann.

to need professional help and/or drug treatment. Symptoms of psychosis are: hallucinations, delusions, confused and disturbed thoughts, a lack of insight and self-awareness. A psychotic episode can arise out of major stress, depression, addiction or an illness such as schizophrenia.

Types of neurotic tendency

Neurotic tendencies fall into four categories or personality types, all of which you will encounter in any church congregation:[7]

- hysterical,
- depressive,
- obsessive compulsive,
- schizoid.

All these tendencies have their particular positives as well as their particular problems. The categories are not mutually exclusive, and as you read you may recognize aspects of yourself in all of them.

The hysterical tendency

In everyday language, hysterical behaviour means an excess of surface emotion. The classic symptoms of hysterical blindness or paralysis, where patients become literally unable to see or to move with there being no physiological basis for it, are now rare, but hysterical behaviour is not.[8] So-called hysterical behaviour – headaches, crying fits, stomach upsets and so on – may attract a lot of attention and sympathy, but it does not get help for the actual problem. In a pastoral situation, it may be that everyone gets mobilized to run around sending emails, writing notes, rearranging themselves to help – and eventually become exasperated because nothing changes. Meanwhile,

---

7 Anthony Storr, 1989, *The Art of Psychotherapy*, London: Secker and Warburg/Heinemann.

8 Cases of hysteria of the former kind formed much of the basis of early psychoanalytic investigation. A severe mental conflict produces an extreme bodily reaction which is not caused by a physical illness, and is cured by getting to the root of the conflict. It is a highly developed form of somatizing.

the person concerned, who seems to have somehow managed to sail through this unchanged, accuses the 'helpers' of coldness and rejection. In extreme distress, this kind of person may resort to a careful suicide attempt. Should you be involved as a pastor, be prepared for medical staff to react unsympathetically, since from their point of view it takes up valuable time and resources.

Unfortunately, all the symptoms and attention-seeking behaviour tend to draw attention away from the part that really needs help. As the analyst David Malan puts it, 'One of the characteristics of a hysterical patient is the subtle quality of appearing to *act* what are nevertheless genuine emotions – a kind of emotional "lying the truth". '[9] The trouble is that although the emotions are genuine they come across as 'crying wolf' because they do not express the real problem. What makes life particularly difficult is that the person themselves is unaware of what their excess of emotion is really expressing.

People with hysterical tendency are often highly creative, anxious to please and have great charm. They may complain that they are good at initial contact but do not have long-term friendships. Intimacy is usually difficult for them, and the lack of it feels like rejection. In a church context, they may be theatrical, get into intense relationships and then wear people out by their demands. While fearful of losing people, they will often expect others to do all the work in maintaining relationships with them.

Pastorally, hysterical behaviour can be hard to put up with. If someone is constantly testing you and acting out, you will need to balance consistency with setting limits: 'Yes I do care about you, but that does not mean I am prepared to stay up talking until two o'clock every morning.'

Yet, the hysterical personality type also has important virtues which are highly valuable if they can be harnessed. They are often energetic, entertaining and fun, and good at raising enthusiasm for projects. They also have a powerful sense of justice, and since they are not afraid of expressing emotion, they will be ready to confront injustice, when they perceive it.

---

9 David Malan, 1995, *Individual Psychotherapy and the Science of Psychodynamics*, 2nd edn, London: Hachette, Ch. 19.

The depressive personality

The following chapter on depression goes into this more deeply, but in a pastoral context it is worth remembering that a depressive tendency often involves aggression turned against oneself: there may be an underlying hostility of which the person themselves is not aware, as well as low self-esteem and a sense of helplessness leading to passivity. A passive dependent person will find it difficult to do anything for himself, while a passive aggressive person will find it impossible to express aggression so will insist on shouldering all the burdens with a heavy sigh.

In a pastoral context, this low sense of self may go with being very self-giving and alert to the needs of others. Such a person may need help to realize that they too need some care.

The obsessive compulsive tendency

Obsessive compulsive people are very orderly, obstinate and parsimonious and are sticklers for rules and regulations. They can be very good at intellectualizing but not much good at feelings and will be drawn to dogma and morality rather than mysticism or charism. Such a person may come from a very authoritarian background and need encouragement to let go of the 'oughts' built into their personality.

They may be scrupulously honest and reliable but also lack flexibility – both experiencing and generating anxiety because of an underlying fear of their own aggression and a great desire for control. As secretary of the PCC, they may insist on getting every last detail of the minutes correct and all the protocol of the meetings exactly right. On the other hand, they will generally be steady and reliable and pay great attention to detail.

The schizoid tendency

A person with schizoid tendencies compartmentalizes their feelings. They are usually deeply frightened of intimacy, though may mask this very successfully in social interactions.

Fear of intimacy may stem from childhood loss and being afraid of starting a relationship for fear of losing it. Or it may come from a fear of being dominated: this person can only retain a sense of self by keeping a distance. Their life experience may well be that other people are so oblivious of their needs that they might as well not exist. In Kafka's novels for example, there is a complete inability to influence authority. Kafka always felt inadequate and somehow wrong in relation to his father. In his religious attitude, there is an Absolute – but it is so remote that a lack of comprehension is inevitable. Where parents have made a child feel that his or her needs are an unbearable imposition, there may be a great deal of buried anger.

In order to cope with social situations and the lack of intimacy, a schizoid person may often construct a fantasy role in which they are superior and thus appear cold, haughty and unapproachable. They may also make virtuous decisions and strive to behave in accordance with certain principles, without having the emotional resources to back this up, as in, 'If I give away all my possessions, and if I hand over my body so that I may boast, but do not have love I gain nothing' (1 Cor. 13.3). The real sadness is that it can be very difficult to conceive of being loved.

A schizoid personality can be an advantage to abstract thinkers. In pastoral situations, a schizoid tendency may be helpful in avoiding getting caught up in the messiness of human relationships and being able to analyse – and name – just what is going on.

Psychosis

All of us have neurotic tendencies of one kind or another. We also have blind spots, which can develop into psychotic episodes. In neurosis, we are aware of feeling ill or disturbed, but in psychosis, we lose at least some of the ability to distinguish between fantasy and reality. For example, a neurotic person may compulsively perform a ritual such as obsessive hand washing, but they will be aware it is pointless, even if they need to do it. A psychotic person is not generally able to evaluate thoughts in this way. Delusions and moods are acted upon, and this is why people with extreme forms of psychosis are dangerous to themselves and to others.

It is often said that the hallmark of psychosis is that the person lacks insight, and while this is largely true, sometimes people can be painfully aware that they are inhabiting a landscape that lacks ordinary reality.

Some features of psychosis are:

- a different view of reality, which it is hard for another person to engage with,
- lack of insight,
- irrational thoughts,
- hearing voices,
- experiencing one's thoughts being controlled or stolen,
- delusions experienced as real.

Psychosis may be due to an illness, or it may be triggered by drug use or a traumatic event. It is not usually, at least in the acute stages, treatable by counselling, though sometimes counselling support may be helpful in enabling a person to keep with their treatment programme or talk about the problems their psychosis is causing for themselves and their family. The psychosis itself will usually be treated by drugs and maybe deep psychotherapy. One of the main problems for families and communities is that many anti-psychotic drugs produce unpleasant side effects.

When and how can you help?

The resolution of many mental health problems lies beyond the reach of pastoral intervention, but this does not mean that certain kinds of support may not be very valuable indeed, and this includes practical as well as emotional support. Therapists, psychiatrists and hospitals do not have all the answers, and some professionals very much welcome contact with a pastoral worker in helping to support patients.

These are some useful questions you can ask yourself if you are wondering whether you can help someone:

- Is this person bringing me a problem I have some experience of or understand quite well?
- Is this person bringing me a problem I have no experience of but can imagine or relate to?

- Is this person simply boring me? – in which case they may be bringing you something that is simply not the real issue or may have tipped over into a disassociated state themselves.
- Is this person ordinarily quite stable but currently under abnormal pressure or in crisis?
- Does this person's problem stem principally from their own way of dealing with the world? If so, do they seem to be in a neurotic or a psychotic state? If the latter, they may need medication and/or psychiatric help.
- Does this person seem dangerous or suicidal? If so, try to get them to seek medical help or consult a professional yourself for advice.

Depression

Depression is often called 'the common cold of mental health'. Most people have some understanding of what it means to be depressed, just as everyone knows what a cold is. Similarly, just as not everyone develops pneumonia or even flu, not everyone will experience depression in its severe and disabling forms. Because it is such a varied and pervasive illness, this will be a long chapter: we will take time and space to explore its many aspects.

Depression and its symptoms
Depression is a wide-ranging illness that affects people in different ways. There is no doubt that some people are more prone to it than others. It is also the case that while some people may experience depression in reaction to particular events such as a loss, others experience it with varying severity in some form or other throughout their lives.

Because of this, psychologists often distinguish between what is called *reactive* depression (a response to a particular event) and *endogenous* depression (an illness a person suffers from whatever their circumstances). This distinction can be helpful as long as we do not treat it too rigidly.

A person suffering from a reactive depression may experience any or all of the symptoms, but their general mood will be responsive to events. For example, they might be cheered up by company, an outing, passing an exam.

In so-called endogenous depression, a person may well have more of the physical symptoms, and depression is a recurrent, life-long problem. It may be associated with bipolar disorder, where depression alternates with periods when the person gets high and believes anything is possible. She or he may become wired up and talkative; in extreme cases they might go out and spend all the family money on a crazy scheme.

Whatever depression is, it has been with us a long time: all its psychological and spiritual symptoms are found in the psalms:

- Low mood, sadness, weariness, a sense of loss: *I am utterly bowed down and prostrate; all day long I go around mourning* (38.6).
- Feeling trapped or anxious: *O Lord, heal me, for my bones are shaking with terror. My soul also is struck with terror* (6.2–3).
- Guilt, self-hatred: *My iniquities have gone over my head; they weigh like a burden too heavy for me. My wounds grow foul and fester because of my foolishness* (38.4–5).
- Feeling lonely, isolated or even alienated: *My friends and companions stand aloof from my affliction, and my neighbours stand afar off* (38.11).
- Losing interest in your surroundings, everything seems futile: *Surely everyone stands as a mere breath. Surely everyone goes about like a shadow. Surely for nothing they are in turmoil; they heap up, and do not know how to gather* (39.5–6).
- Feeling helpless: *I am like the deaf, I do not hear; like the mute who cannot speak.* (38.13).
- Having no energy: *I am poured out like water, and all my bones are out of joint* (22.14).
- Feeling irritable or resentful: *I lie down among lions that greedily devour human prey; their teeth are spears and arrows, their tongues sharp swords* (57.4).
- A sense of being abandoned: *My God, my God, why hast thou forsaken me and art so far from my help and from the voice of my complaint?* (22.1).
- A preoccupation with death, which may include both dread of death and longing for it: *My heart is in anguish within me, the terrors of death have fallen upon me* (55.4). *Lord, let me know my end, and what is the measure of my days; let me know how fleeting my life is* (39.4).

One corollary of this is that the psalms can help a depressed person to feel less alone. They can also be a way into prayer, which itself can be very difficult when you are depressed. Psalms 22, 38, 39 and 55 are particularly relevant, but there are many more that you can search out, or encourage others to search out for themselves.

The symptoms of depression are often physical as well as psychological and spiritual:

- tiredness, lethargy,
- sleep disturbance, especially waking up in the small hours of the morning,
- panic attacks,
- loss of appetite (not only for food but for life itself), or comfort eating,
- increase in consumption of alcohol or other drugs,
- loss of sexual desire or function.

Depression can also affect memory and concentration and may even lead to delusional states or hallucinations.

Some underlying causes of depression

Where depression comes from and how it lifts remains largely mysterious in spite of a huge body of research into its causes and treatments. Most people fall into one of two camps: some maintain that depression is the result of a chemical deficiency; others that depression is a sign of some deep unresolved conflict and that the way through it is to explore your inner world to find the root of that conflict.

These two approaches are, of course, not mutually exclusive, and we would not expect them to be if the human being is an integrated whole of body, mind and spirit. We know well that the biochemistry of the brain is affected by experience, and also that drugs can sometimes alleviate the symptoms of depression. When they work well, they may provide an essential protection against the symptoms that enables a person get through, or even to do the inner work necessary for recovery. Again, depression itself can have a protective function when something really terrible has happened,: it dampens down responses until a person is ready to deal with the feelings.

Where there is no obvious triggering event, both physical and psychological factors may be involved, including:

- bipolar disorder or other depressive illness,
- other cyclical patterns,
- childhood trauma that has not been recognized or processed,
- loss or unresolved inner conflict,
- depression in the family,
- irrational guilt,
- insufficient filters against existential anxiety.

Bipolar disorder

What we now call bipolar disorder and used to call 'manic depression' is characterized by mood swings which can last for weeks or months at a time. A diagnosis can be reassuring for the sufferer and their family, and if the cycle is identified, drugs are often a help in managing it. Particularly during 'up' periods, however, people with bipolar disorder are often resistant to drugs or therapy and may need help in making sure that treatment is maintained. Drugs also need to be monitored as they are potential aids to suicide.

People with bipolar disorder are often highly creative, deep depression alternating with bursts of creative output. The illness itself and its effect on the family are masterfully described in Patrick Gale's novel, *Notes from an Exhibition*. Two characters in the novel suffer from bipolar disorder, and through them Gale describes the illness in some detail. Rachel is a highly talented artist, whose creative periods alternate with suicidal depression often involving hospital admissions. Morwenna, her daughter, lives a rootless, wandering life, which is nevertheless her own way of coping:

[Morwenna] was intelligent and well-educated and had diagnosed herself . . . long before any doctor . . . She had tried medication and rejected it. For personal reasons which her coolest, most rational moments showed her to be justified, she had chosen to surrender to her illness . . . She had learned to manage herself.

When she was entering a high but was not yet in a dangerous, hypo-manic state, she stored up messages for herself to help pull herself through the dark times. She wrote stories, poetry or simply long letters to herself, e-mailing copies of them to an address maintained for her by a convent which had once taken her in.[1]

Gale also skilfully charts the effects of the illness on the men in the family: Rachel's husband and Morwenna's brothers, all of whom, while not sufferers themselves, learn different ways of living with it. The novel is in part a tribute to a close friend who had bipolar disorder and eventually killed himself: 'Like most suicides,' writes Gale, 'his death stirred up relentless cycles of guilt and anger in me, which not even writing this novel has put to rest. But at least I got to weave my own sort of wreath for him.'[2]

Other cyclical patterns

The world we live in is governed by cycles of time and season, and our lives are bound into them. This is reflected, of course, in the liturgical life of the church.

Some people are powerfully affected by seasons: the darkness of winter, the bitter-sweet beauty of the spring, the glare of summer or the fading of autumn. Identifying depression and its triggers does not make it go away, but it can provide hope that it will pass, and even help a person to prepare for its onslaught.

Likewise, the liturgical seasons weave themselves into our stories. It is not uncommon for Lent to trigger depression. Christmas, falling at the darkest time of the year, and with its strong associations with family and childhood, is also a time when people are particularly vulnerable. If someone's depression seems to be cyclical or season dependent, it may be worth checking out what associations there are with that time of the year.

Jackie, a keen choir member, was upset that she always seemed to hit a depression at Easter. The Easter hymns reduced her to tears, and this also made her feel guilty: 'This is supposed to be the most joyful time of the year, and I can't feel it.' When Jackie was ten, her

---

1 P. Gale, 2007, *Notes from an Exhibition*, London: Harper, p. 260.
2 Gale, *Notes*, 'P.S. Ideas, interviews and features', p. 9.

much-loved grandmother had died – on Easter Day. As she talked about this, she realized that no one had expected her, as a child, to grieve. Her mother, devastated by her own mother's death, had withdrawn into her own grief, leaving Jackie emotionally stranded.

Moreover, Jackie's grandmother died at the family home, and helping her mother care for her had been a time of great intimacy and a kind of 'cosiness'. No one had prepared her for it ending in death. For her, then, Easter became associated with sudden loss and abandonment. Jackie began to acknowledge that singing Easter hymns made her angry. Christ might be risen, but that had not helped her grandmother. Yet, her own anger terrified her, and she was often reduced to tears instead of allowing herself to be angry. Over time, she was able to experience the childhood grief that had been blocked and find compassion towards her own angry response. Easter acquired new meaning: her grandmother's death was still real, but so was the hope of resurrection, and she could begin to understand this as the adult she had become.

Another powerful cycle is the hormonal one that affects women in particular. Talking about this is often frowned upon, because it can be used by employers as a reason to discriminate against women. There is little doubt, however, that a small percentage of women (about 3–8 per cent) suffer from premenstrual dysphoric disorder (PMDD), and the insistence that this does not happen makes it worse.

Ceri was generally content with her life, doing well at work and in a long-term-loving relationship. Nevertheless, the rhythm of her life was regularly railroaded by unmanageable mental and physical distress. She is someone who has been able to benefit from drug therapy and she was immensely relieved when her GP recognized PMDD and prescribed anti-depressants:

> You can suffer from PMDD if you have it yourself or if you have to live with someone who does. Either way, it's awful . . . Does the patient, regularly each month, wake up unable to stop crying long enough to get to work? Does she scream, yell, physically attack loved ones? . . . Does she have to refuse party invitations and plan holidays to fit around the week of madness? . . . You know it isn't you. You can't help it. You lose the skin that enables you to carry on through daily life.

> Some people . . . have challenged the labelling of this as a disor-
> der [but it] *needs* labelling so that it can be dealt with. A label is
> the first step to the medical establishment taking it seriously . . .
> [A low dose of SSRIs is like] water-wings. Like a life-belt . . . I
> can't believe I've wasted years of my life being a monster, when
> it's so easy to fix.[3]

Similarly, some women are particularly susceptible to post-natal
depression, while others find the menopause a massive emotional
upheaval. While we should not assume all women are subject to
these difficulties, it is important to acknowledge that they are very
real for some, not least because they make people feel terribly
guilty: 'How can I keep turning on the husband who loves me?'
'How can I fail to love this baby?' and so on. In church circles,
these problems are often glossed over, increasing the sufferer's
sense of isolation and guilt. A pastor who can acknowledge the
reality of the depression and encourage the sufferer – and her husband or partner – to talk to their GP or seek other help is already
alleviating these secondary difficulties.

Childhood trauma that has not been recognized or processed
We have already touched on the fact that extreme childhood trauma
such as violence or sexual abuse can lead to depression in adult
life. More everyday experiences can have the same effect.

At 29, Robin was doing well as an IT consultant, but he began
to suffer from bouts of depression in which he was overcome by
self-doubt. His father, an upwardly mobile businessman, had sent
Robin to boarding school at the age of seven. Here Robin had
been isolated, out of place and often bullied. He experienced himself as a commodity – used by his father to satisfy social ambition.
His mother, though aware that he was unhappy, had not had the
strength to confront his father about this. She felt depressed and
guilty that she had not done so.

In adult life, Robin was driven by a need to satisfy his father's
ambitions for him – and also to protect his mother, who was
unable to express her own needs. In counselling, he was able to

---

3 Private communication, unpublished.

name how awful boarding school had been. While he still got depressed, he felt less helpless in relation to it. He was able to distinguish between the feelings from the past which belonged to schooldays and those in the present which belonged to his current situation. He also began to differentiate himself from both his parents. Having managed to own his depression, he could see his mother's situation more clearly and as separate from his own.

Loss or unresolved inner conflict

In this section, we shall look in some detail at different aspects of depression as perceived by sufferers and professionals.

For Andrew Solomon, himself a lifelong sufferer, a capacity for depression is a corollary of our ability to love:

> Depression is the flaw in love. To be creatures who love, we must be creatures who can despair at what we lose, and depression is the mechanism of that despair . . . Love . . . is what cushions the mind and protects it from itself . . . Love forsakes us from time to time, and we forsake love. In depression, the meaninglessness of every enterprise and every emotion, the meaninglessness of life itself, becomes self-evident. The only feeling left in the loveless state is insignificance.[4]

Depression triggered by loss is different from sadness or grieving. In depression, the feelings are so unmanageable that all your energy goes into suppressing them – hence the loss of energy and sense of everything shutting down.

It is not always obvious what the loss is. Freud recognized that in depression you are mourning a loss that is not obvious either to you or to the people around you:

> the primary loss is not the lost object but a loss of your own self-esteem. The loss becomes a matter of self-reproach, which according to Freud masks reproach of a person one loves,

---

4 Andrew Solomon, 2001, *The Noonday Demon*, London: Chatto and Windus 2001, p. 15.

has loved or ought to love – so the anger gets turned against oneself.[5]

The poet Gwyneth Lewis, who suffered from severe depression herself, argues that the only cure is the truth:

Approached in a certain way, depression is a lie detector of last resort. By knocking you out for a while, it allows you to ditch the out-of-date ideas by which you've been living and to grasp a more accurate description of the terrain . . . If you can cope with the internal nuclear winter of depression and come through it without committing suicide – the disease's most serious side effect – then, in my experience, depression can be a great friend.[6]

Similarly, drawing on her experience as a psychotherapist, Emmy Gut argues that the way through depression is to find the roots of inner conflict.[7] She uses Asher Lev in the novel by Chaim Potok as a case study.[8] When he is six, Asher's mother, Rivkeh, has a severe crisis when her brother, Yaakov, dies. Yaakov had become Rivkeh's protector after their parents were killed in a car crash when they were children. She married young and has one child, Asher. An intelligent, deeply religious person, she is happy in her marriage, but because her husband has to travel as an assistant to the rabbi, Yaakov's support remains important.

When Yaakov suddenly dies in an accident at the age of 27, Rivkeh has a fit of continuous screaming and is taken to hospital. She returns completely withdrawn: she sleeps, lies in bed, smokes. Only once does she become aware of Asher, and urges him to paint pretty things. In time, she recovers and declares that Yaakov

---

5 Sigmund Freud, 1917, 'Mourning and Melancholic States', in J. Rickman (ed.), 1957, *A General Selection from the Works of Sigmund Freud*, New York: Liveright, p. 128.

6 Gwyneth Lewis, 2002, *Sunbathing in the Rain: A Cheerful Book about Depression*, London: Flamingo, p. xv.

7 Emmy Gut, 1989, *Productive and Unproductive Depression*, London: Tavistock/Routledge.

8 Chaim Potok, 1973, My *Name is Asher Lev*, London: Penguin.

is dead, but his work must carry on: she will enter college and take up the same studies. She functions, but is never the same cheerful companion she used to be. Asher himself becomes increasingly depressed.

Gut argues that Yaakov's death triggers the unmourned loss of Rivkeh's parents. Like Jackie, who could not bear the Easter hymns after her grandmother died, she was given no help with her grief. When Yaakov dies, she becomes like a helpless, disoriented child, and her only hope is a powerful identification with him: a compromise between her need for him and her need to care for her husband and son. Asher is a gifted painter, and in adolescence, he is torn between art and religion. He cannot satisfy either without destroying the other so he does nothing and becomes badly depressed. His father is sent abroad to work but Asher and his mother stay home because Asher cannot cope with the move. Eventually he produces a picture of his mother crucified between himself and his father – a travesty of Jesus on the cross with Mary and John. It is a deep attack on his own Jewish roots, and causes immense shock in the community, but he has made the break necessary to become himself.

Depression in the family

It is highly likely that there is a genetic component to a tendency to depression. At the same time, growing up with depression can condition us to respond in that way under stress.

The Asher Lev story shows how depression can also work systemically in a family. Gwyneth Lewis feels 'fierce about this because our family . . . allowed itself to be dictated to by my mother's depression'. As often happens in a family where one member has a severe mental health problem, they learned 'not to be too insistent in [our] emotions because my mother's reaction might be too hot to handle'. She concludes:

> The depressed person should be allowed all the space in the world and a safe place in which to go through the worst of their suffering. But they shouldn't take over the whole house . . . Children, especially, should be encouraged to carry on as usual, told not to feel guilty about their mother or father [or sibling]

being ill, and that . . . the best thing that they can do to help is to remain cheerful themselves . . . They need to identify a cut-off point to enable themselves to maintain emotional autonomy. This doesn't mean being unsympathetic or harsh towards the patient but it does mean not giving your own life as a hostage to hell.[9]

As a pastor, you are likely to know the other people suffering from the depression – close friends and family members. Be aware of the strain that this can be for them, encourage them to talk about it and if possible share with others in the same situation. There is often little anyone can do but wait for it to pass, and the lack of recovery in the face of loving care and patience can feel like a major rejection.

It can, then, be very hard to maintain compassion and however patient family members may be there are likely to be frustration and anger lurking somewhere in their response to it all. The people closest to a depressed person are often angry at the remoteness of the person they love, at the waste of life. It is common to feel dragged down or helpless, and anger is also a survival mechanism against the pull into the void. A pastor may be in the privileged position of knowing the whole family and able to give the opportunity for these feelings to be acknowledged.

Irrational guilt

Depression is also closely associated with guilt and can exacerbate it: 'I shouldn't feel like this, because I have so many good things and other people are starving/lonely/living in war zones . . .'

It may also arise out of a problem far in the past that has left a legacy of guilt over something that could not be solved. For example, Emily was the younger sister of a man who had been brain damaged at birth. She grew up with his many problems and mood swings, her mother's stress and despair, her father's growing alcoholism. She could do nothing to save her family from falling apart, and as an adult she was tormented by guilt and depression. The very thing that should have been a joy – her own healthy birth –

---

9 Lewis, *Sunbathing*, pp. 139ff.

was experienced as something she had stolen from her brother, even though she had not even been conceived when he was born.

The effects of a sibling who has been damaged in some way should never be underestimated, however well-intentioned the parents. An exceptional account of one person's experience is *The Music Room* by William Fiennes.[10]

Insufficient filters against existential anxiety

Freud observed that people with a propensity for melancholia have 'a keener eye for truth than others who are not melancholic'.[11]

As Solomon puts it, 'It is arguably the case that depressed people have a more accurate view of the world around them than do non-depressed people.'[12] If a person prone to depression has insufficient filters against reality, they may experience a level of pain that would be better kept under control. On the other hand, it is unreal to filter out the world too much. Solomon points out that optimism about the world and oneself is not an evolutionary priority: 'People who don't have enough anxiety and sadness to keep them out of trouble . . . are too cheerful, too fearless, and they are not kind.'[13] Quoting the French psychiatrist Julia Kristeva, who suggested that depression is sometimes a shield against madness, he writes, 'Perhaps it is easier to say simply that we rely on our sorrows more than we know.'[14]

Treatment

There are three main treatments for depression:

- drugs,
- counselling and psychotherapy,
- as a last resort, electroconvulsive shock treatment is still occasionally used.

---

10 W. Fiennes, 2009, *The Music Room*, London: Picador.
11 Freud, 'Mourning'.
12 Solomon, *Noonday Demon*, p. 433.
13 Solomon, *Noonday Demon*, p. 434.
14 Solomon, *Noonday Demon*, p. 435.

The first two are not mutually exclusive and may be used concurrently.

Drugs

There are many different kinds of anti-depressant. For a thorough overview see Solomon's book, *The Noonday Demon*, where he also discusses counselling and psychotherapy.

One of the biggest issues is that many people dislike the idea of taking drugs. They may feel they should be able to find spiritual resources to overcome depression, or be afraid that they will lose their identity or their creative ability if they start taking drugs that affect the brain. They may also be afraid of becoming addicted. As a pastor, it is important to be aware that drugs can help to alleviate the symptoms sufficiently to allow a person to function, or even to be able to work on the depression in other ways. They can also act as a protection, when a person is preoccupied with suicidal thoughts.

At the same time, people have strong individual reactions to anti-depressant drugs. Side effects can include violent mood swings or even an increased risk of suicide, and it is possible to get hooked. Not all doctors are responsible about prescribing. If someone does start a course of anti-depressants, it is important that they are monitored every few months, rather than just receiving repeat prescriptions. If one drug does not work, there are others that can be tried.

Counselling and psychotherapy

In counselling or psychotherapy, a person will be encouraged to recognize their depression, and work with it.

A cognitive behavioural approach will analyse the thoughts and associations a person has, and help them to find strategies for dealing with their depression. Other approaches will explore experiences and buried memories that may lie behind it.

Electroconvulsive therapy

Electroconvulsive therapy (ECT), where electrodes are attached to the sides of the head and an electric shock passed through the brain is rarely used today, but still exists as a last resort. The idea of this treatment can be very frightening for both patient and relatives. It is still not known why it works, but sometimes it does. It also often results in short-term memory loss, which can be distressing.

The pastoral response

Depression is such a pervasive – if not universal – phenomenon, that it perhaps highlights the participatory nature of pastoral action. One of the difficult things about trying to help a depressed person is its infectious nature. We can easily feel pulled down into the depression – or find ourselves fighting desperately to get out.

When coping with depression – your own or someone else's – it is vital to remember that depressions do lift and may even hold the seeds to recovery. If the inner self can be questioned with kindness, this can be the beginning of processing experience that has previously been simply impossible to deal with. We can see echoes of this in the psalms quoted at the beginning of this chapter. Having voiced his despair, the psalmist often seems, without any explanation, to recover his faith in and relationship with God.

One thing that does not help is trying to cheer up a depressed person. They will already be feeling bad about how they feel and do not need to be made to feel worse. What you can do is be prepared to stay around without having any major expectations, but trusting that sooner or later something will change. Maggie Robbins, herself a sufferer from bipolar disorder, volunteered at a hostel for people with AIDS. She found them unresponsive to her attempts to chat, and this was difficult:

> Then it hit me: these guys aren't going to make small talk. In fact . . . they weren't going to talk at all. But they didn't want me to leave. So I decided, I'm here with them and I'm going to be with them . . . So I just stayed with them that afternoon, without talking. The loving is that you are there, simply paying attention, unconditionally. If suffering is what a person is doing right then, that's what they're doing. You're being with that – not trying like crazy to do something about it. I've learned how to do that.[15]

---

15 Solomon, *Noonday Demon*, p. 437.

There is a hidden spirituality in depression, and many people have found meaning in this. It may be experienced as a creative darkness that insulates them from the outside world while a process takes place within. The lifting of depression can also be a resurrection experience, and something to remember and hold on to if the depression recurs. In its positive aspect, depression teaches us about the unavoidability of loss, and coming through it may help us to find the ability to mourn, which is so essential to mental health. It can isolate us, but it can also cut through our ordinary defences to open up new doors of compassion in the soul.

Kate, for example, was a highly competent woman, who always seemed in control of her own life and those around her. After a miscarriage, she was deeply depressed for several months. Afterwards she said that the experience, horrible though it was, had introduced her to the human race. She still liked to organize and manage, but she had a new understanding of people who simply wanted to let be.

It is not helpful, of course, to tell a person that they should be finding meaning in their depression, but people do find resources in the psalms and in Bible stories. It may be worth asking what stories are meaningful to them, and why.

John, for example, often read in church, and in particular he always asked if he could read when the story of Jonah and the bush came round in the lectionary (Jonah 4).

This passage follows on after the whale, after Jonah has unsuccessfully preached to the people of Nineveh, and in particular after God has not punished the people of Nineveh as he had said he would do. Jonah feels thoroughly let down and angry. He tells God, 'It would be better for me to die than to live' and goes out into the desert. God provides a bush to shelter him, but the next day provides a worm that destroys the bush. In the relentless heat of the sun, Jonah once more asks to die. 'You are concerned about the bush,' says God, 'for which you did not labour. Should I not be concerned for Nineveh in which there are more than a hundred and twenty thousand people?'

One day, John's vicar asked him why he liked to read this story in church, and John explained that there had been a point in his life when he desperately wanted to be ordained and spread the gospel. When he was not accepted for ordination he fell into a major depression, and it took him a long time to get in touch with his own anger and frustration with God over this. In the story, Jonah models a relationship with God that he himself had been afraid of having, when he became ill: he is able to protest and argue – and he also comes to terms with his own helplessness. At the same time, John also felt that God's compassion for Nineveh renewed his own faith that he could trust God to guide him in the journey that was right for him.

Suicidal thoughts and actions

In severe depression, of course, suicidal thoughts represent a serious risk to life. Always take suicidal thoughts seriously. It is not true that talking about it means the person will not go ahead and do it, but it often helps. There is a link between suicide and age.

Young males in particular are at increased risk, although young females make more suicide attempts. Suicide rates level out for 30–40 year olds and then climb with increased age. When people reach 55, they are at a higher risk of taking their life, and this becomes even more apparent in the 75-plus age group.[16]

Paradoxically the risk of an actual attempt is greatest as recovery from depression begins, when a person no longer feels completely helpless, and is beginning to get some energy back – and may well feel they never want to go through that again.

As well as being available to listen, it is worth checking if you or someone else can be of practical help. If, for example, you think someone might take an overdose, encourage them not to keep large supplies of pills in the house, and maybe even to find someone who will look after stocks of painkillers and sleeping pills for them. Encourage them to talk to their GP about it, so that they can be careful about prescriptions.

The Samaritans are a great resource. Get to know your local group, so that you understand what happens when someone rings them – or at least familiarize yourself through their excellent website: www.samaritans.org

---

16 Maggie Helen, 2002, *Coping with Suicide*, London: Sheldon Press, p. 19.

Always talk to a supervisor or trusted professional, if you are anxious about a possible suicide. It may not be possible to go into detail if there are issues of confidentiality, but it is vital to reality check your own anxieties.

Many people, of course, think about, plan and get close to taking their own lives yet still manage to stay alive. We cannot predict what will bring someone back from the brink. It may be some small obstacle that gets in the way: the pharmacy or off-licence is unexpectedly shut perhaps, or a passer-by interrupts a reverie on a bridge while you are contemplating a jump.

Occasionally, getting really close to actually killing yourself seems to trigger an opposite reaction, as William Styron describes in his remarkable memoir of depression, *Darkness Visible*.[17] He first pays tribute to a number of other writers whose lives ended in suicide, and then goes on to describe how close he came to it himself.

Many kinds of drugs and psychotherapy having failed to cure his depression, he carefully makes all the preparations to kill himself. That night, after his wife has gone to bed, he sits downstairs on what he believes to be his last night alive and forces himself to watch a film which includes an actress who had acted in one of his own plays. The film is set in late nineteenth-century Boston and, at one point, as the characters walk through a music conservatory, the music turns to a soaring passage from Brahms' Alto Rhapsody.

Although he had been unable to respond to any music for months, this music, as Styron says, 'pierced my heart like a dagger'. He is flooded with the recollection of everything that has happened in that house – 'the children, the festivals, the love and work . . .' – there is a long list – and realizes that this is more than he could ever abandon, just as the memory of his own suicide is more than he could inflict on those close to him. At the same time, he also realizes that he could not inflict it on himself. He wakes his wife and gets himself admitted to hospital.

One point that emerges from this story, of course, is the role that family and friends play in suicidal thoughts. Suicide may be an act of despair, or even of defiance against the universe, but for those

---

17 W. Styron, 1991, *Darkness Visible*, London: Jonathan Cape.

left behind it is usually experienced as a cruel rejection. Styron and his family were fortunate in that he realized he could not inflict the memory of his own suicide on them, but this is not always the case.

For example, Helen was plunged into depression when memories surfaced of abuse in her childhood. She convinced herself that her children, now in their early twenties, would be better off without her. 'I'll write them a note telling them how much I love them,' she thought. 'They will grieve, but in the long term they will be better off.' In the event, Helen did not kill herself, but it is always worth checking out what a person thinks the effect on others will be. It may be that someone simply feels so worthless they cannot believe that they contribute to the lives of those around them. Suicidal thoughts can also be where buried but necessary anger resides: 'Then they'll understand what I went through/what they did to me . . .'

When should you consider getting further help?
Remember that depression is a serious and life-threatening illness. Emmy Gut provides the following checklist to help you decide when professional help may be needed:[18]

- Is our friend having to deal with difficult circumstances, such as marital or family discord; major loss through death or separation; stress at work, economic difficulties or poor health?
- Does our friend also demonstrate anxiety, grief, guilty feelings and self-accusations, shame or anger that is hard to comprehend?
- Has our friend earlier had periods of depression that lasted for some time without resolving themselves in a way that in retrospect made them understandable for both that person and for others? Were any of these periods disabling?

Does it seem difficult for our friend to:
- develop and keep friendship or love relationships,
- to have satisfactory sex relations,

---

18 Gut, *Depression*, p. 207.

- to show a normal range of feelings from joy and affection to those of anger, grief and hatred,
- to be discriminating in who to trust or distrust,
- to succeed at and relish work and keep a job?

In other words, is he or she even without depression not functioning comfortably? If the answer is 'Yes' to the first of these but not the others, this may signal that support is needed with the presenting problem; positive answers to one or more of the others as well as the first may signal a need for professional therapeutic or medical help. If this is the case, a gentle encouragement to allow a person to be helped can be a valuable use of pastoral authority.

If the worst happens, it is important to seek help yourself: any suicide leaves a legacy of guilt for those who tried to care for the person concerned.

II

Addiction

> Once one has experienced the taste of God one can never be satisfied or
> have enough of it.
>
> *Macarian Homilies, V, 86*

For many people, the word addiction is associated with something
that happens to other people: drug addicts, homeless alcoholics
who haunt the local churchyard or bus shelter; people who have a
problem, perhaps, but not particularly our problem.

Yet, the language of addiction also permeates everyday conversation: 'I can't live without . . .'; 'I need a fix of . . . what? Caf-
feine? *The Simpsons*? The news?' Often we adopt the language
of alcohol addiction – chocaholic, workaholic and so on – partly
because of the rhythmic ease with which these words form themselves, but also because alcoholism is a paradigm addiction that
has been with us for a very long time. Because of this, we will take
alcohol addiction as our central paradigm. Alcohol has all the
hallmarks of an addictive substance:

- It eases the pain.
- It relieves the stress of social situations.
- It relieves loneliness and provides a bond with other people.
- It is a good thing, which can gradually turn destructive to
  health, relationships, work.
- Once it has become an end in itself, it tolerates no com-
  petition.

However much an alcoholic may love family and friends, these
cannot compete with the need for alcohol. 'Wine to gladden the

human heart' (Ps. 104.15) turns as sour as the apple picked in Eden. It comes between the addict and human relationships and between the addict and God. This was vividly described by Gerry, a devout priest and recovering alcoholic, who has now been sober for nearly 20 years. 'Whenever I say Psalm 55,' he said, 'it always speaks to me of alcohol – "my companion, my own familiar friend" who betrayed me.'

Addiction and satisfaction

As human beings, we have physical, psychological and spiritual needs, and it is natural that we should seek to fulfil them. We are appetitive beings. Growth and movement are essential to humanity. Far from seeking a state of homeostasis we are drawn onwards by desire and curiosity throughout our lives. We have only to watch the way a baby develops into a small child who can walk and speak and manipulate objects and make relationships to experience the immense energy that drives our lives. This is all part of the spiritual journey whereby we seek God, who is radically unknowable: 'All of us, with unveiled faces, seeing the glory of the Lord as though reflected in a mirror, are being transformed into the same image from one degree of glory to another' (2 Cor. 3.18). This journey is never complete in this life and is expressed physically and emotionally as well as spiritually. It is natural then that the satisfaction of hunger or desire opens up to new hunger or desire. This is what makes us alive.

In a normal cycle, giving nourishment leads to digestion and satisfaction, and makes room for a new desire or hunger to appear (or for the same hunger to recur when there is a need for further nourishment, as in basic needs such as food, water and sleep). See Table 1 overleaf.

The crucial factor in this table is digestion. If we are unable to digest something, whether food or an emotional experience or liturgy, we are unable to be satisfied by it. We cannot reach, even temporarily, that state described by the psalmist: 'I have calmed and quieted my soul, like a weaned child with its mother' – who no longer needs her milk, but has moved on to solid food (Ps. 131.2). Digestion in this sense is an emotional and spiritual

Table 1: A cycle of hunger and satisfaction

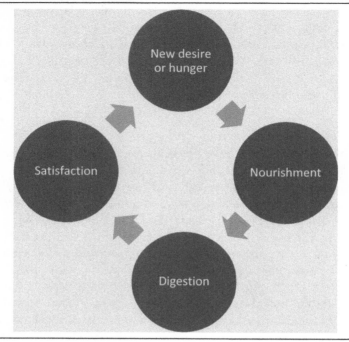

process, without which we end up facing an aching void. In addiction we cannot process nourishment but are left in a state of on-going, unsatisfiable hunger.

Addiction diverts all or some of the nourishment into inner emptiness, so the need is never satisfied. The only effect of the first drink, for example, is to make me want another. See Table 2.

These cycles apply to relationships as well as to physical substances. For some people, the ability to 'digest' – to receive or benefit from a loving relationship – is damaged by failures of attachment earlier on. There are many who nevertheless refuse to give up, and may eventually find something that enables them to build on the meagre resources they have. One such person was Melanie, who had a very low sense of her own worth. Her sense of herself began to flourish with the help of Beth, a priest who was also her spiritual companion. The situation became risky

Table 2: The cycle of hunger and satisfaction interrupted

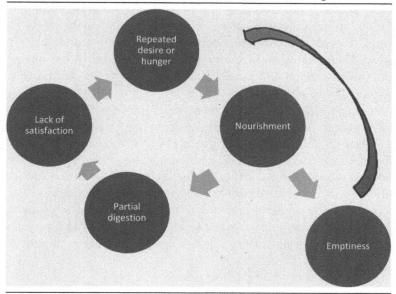

for both of them, because Melanie became psychologically very dependent and needed an immense amount of support and reassurance to hold on to the new sense of herself, and Beth found this very difficult. Nevertheless, she managed to remain consistent and kind, while maintaining her boundaries. She worked hard at this because she believed in Melanie – you might say she was able to nurture the image of God she detected in her, just as she became, for a brief while 'God' for Melanie. Over time Melanie, herself was gradually able to grow into a mutual and equal relationship and became a valuable member of the pastoral team, remaining so when Beth moved on to a new parish. Such dependency on the road to mutuality – or independence – is not addiction. Nor is it unusual. It carries great potential for healing.

It is possible, however, for such relationships to become ends in themselves. Unable to take in and learn to live with the acceptance and love that is offered, a person may become stuck in their need. Their demands become intolerable, relationships break down, and a restless search for the good feeling that sets in during the early stages of a relationship begins. At that point, a person might be said to be addicted to short term, fleetingly gratifying relationships. For pastors, who participate in the life of a community, it should come as no surprise that this can work both ways: one of the most common and powerful addictions is to the gratification involved in being needed by others.

In any addiction there is a downward spiral, whereby the lack of digestion means that more and more is needed in the search for satisfaction. If the addiction is to a physical substance, the body develops 'tolerance' – that is, as time goes on, more and more is needed to get the same effect. In due course, the addiction inevitably begins to interfere with health, work and relationships – and it is at this point that the addict finds him or herself unable to make a choice to change without recognition and help. It is a process noted by Saint Augustine, when he describes the chain of habit:

Out of stubborn will a desire is made.
Out of a desire served a habit is made.
Where a habit is not resisted a necessity is made.[1]

That is, a habit begun in seeking a good thing – relaxation after work for example – becomes a compulsive urge. It becomes less of a good thing when we start to watch the clock at work to get to the drink or spend scarce family money on it or start to get drunk every evening. These things tend to creep up slowly, and one of the major obstacles to recovery is denial. Addicts often go on for years convinced they can kick the habit. It is only when a person realizes that they cannot do this alone that the healing process can begin.

It is not enough, of course, simply to remove the source of any addiction: the addict is left with a terrible and painful emptiness, and in a physical addiction the body may have life-threatening reactions to the deprivation of the substance. It is the emptiness, however, that has to be faced in order to come through.

---

1 Augustine, *Confessions* 8:5.

Addiction and spirituality

Addiction is often thought of as a thirst for God diverted from its true object, and addicts are often very spiritually aware people. This was C. G. Jung's understanding of addiction. For him, the unconscious is far more than some inaccessible part of the human psyche: it is a gateway to the numinous and has a quality of otherness that is a reality, not a fabrication of human imagination. Since it has the power to overwhelm our conscious mind, individually or collectively, it requires our deepest respect. In the 1930s, Jung tried to treat Rowland H., later one of the founder members of Alcoholics Anonymous. When Rowland returned to Jung for more treatment after a relapse, Jung told him that no medical intervention could help him, and his only source of hope was a genuine religious conversion. He advised him to place himself in a religious atmosphere and hope for the best.

Twenty-five years later Bill Wilson, another founder of AA, wrote to thank Jung for 'this candid and humble statement [which] was the first foundation on which our Society has since been built'. In his reply, Jung wrote about Rowland H.: 'his craving for alcohol was the equivalent on a low level of the spiritual thirst of our being for wholeness . . . for the union with God'.[2]

Jung maintains that if we do not make a choice to believe in God as we understand him, something else will take on for us that absolute quality that belongs to God. This may be a substance such as alcohol or heroin or any of the more abstract things we can become addicted to, including religion itself. Any of these things can come between our capacity for belief, awe and devotion and the God to whom these things rightfully belong: it is precisely because something has captured our deepest spiritual devotion that it becomes an absolute. It is also why the experience of those closest to an addict is that in any contest they will lose. A workaholic, for example, may love his family dearly, but being in bondage to his career will always put work before their needs. According to Jung, anything that is in this sense inescapable

---

2 Letter from C. G. Jung to Bill Wilson, 1961. Quoted in *Pass It On: the Story of Bill Wilson and How the AA Message Reached the World*, published by Alcoholics Anonymous.

becomes God for us, unless we are able to choose to set something equally strong against it:

> [We are] free to decide whether God shall be a 'spirit' or a natural phenomenon like the craving of a morphine addict, and hence whether 'God' shall act as a beneficent or a destructive force.[3]

This is well understood by Alcoholics Anonymous, whose core principle is that the individual alcoholic is powerless over alcohol. Only by handing his or her life over to God, however God might be understood, or to a 'Higher Power' is recovery possible. AA fights free of dogmatic language, out of respect for those who have been damaged or alienated from God by their experience of religion. Nevertheless, the ongoing struggle to surrender the will is central to the programme: it is part of the disease of alcoholism (as well as a commonplace human reaction) to make more and more desperate attempts to take control when things get difficult.

Most people find it difficult to relinquish control of their lives, and when they have not been properly cared for in early life and have taken premature responsibility for themselves, the idea of surrendering the will can be particularly threatening. Yet, according to AA, this is the first step on the path to freedom: 'The more we become willing to depend on a higher power, the more independent we actually are.'[4] This freedom is compared to that of a person who lives in a house equipped with a supply of electricity. Our simple daily needs are met by an energy that few of us understand or are even aware of, and this releases us into comfort, security and personal independence. To tinker with the electrics ourselves, however, can be extremely dangerous. For the addict, then, reliance needs to replace defiance.

These passages were brought to my attention by Christine, a recovering alcoholic who was facing a situation that she had

---

3 C. G. Jung, 1938, *Psychology and Religion*, New Haven: Yale University Press.

4 *Twelve Steps and Twelve Traditions*, 1952, Alcoholics Anonymous General Office, Step 3, p. 37.

previously tried to drown in alcohol. Her drinking had been tied up with fear that God would expect of her something she could not do, that she would be required to make a decision she could not make. She described how difficult it was in sobriety to go on trusting God's will as leading her into freedom. The temptation was to take a rational stance and foreclose on her dilemma rather than waiting to see where God might be taking her. She found courage in the Serenity Prayer said daily by AA members:

> God grant me the serenity to accept the things I cannot change, courage to change the things I can, and the wisdom to know the difference.

A potential for addiction, then, is also a potential for seeking God: the 'restless heart' described by Augustine.[5] The mystic, the artist and the addict all descend into the depths, but the addict is held hostage there. All three, as in the case of Dostoevsky, may be the same person.

The physical and psychological roots of addiction

Spiritual hunger may lie at the root of our propensity for addiction, but for any individual there are a number of physical and psychological risk factors. No one of these will necessarily predispose you to addiction on its own, but in interaction with each other they become very powerful. The five main factors are:

- **Physical make-up**, including your genetic inheritance. Some people are more physiologically vulnerable because of the way their bodies metabolize alcohol and other addictive substances. This is why alcoholism and other addictions run in families, but not all family members are equally at risk (though this does not mean that those who are less at risk are immune).
- **Culture:** the kind of people you mix with and the work you do, media and advertising, religious attitudes to drugs

---

5 'Our hearts are restless till they rest in thee' – Augustine, *Confessions*.

and alcohol. In some professions, drinking is almost a requirement. Barry was very pleased to obtain his first 'proper' job as a university lecturer in engineering. Half-way through his first summer in the job, he was refusing to drink at all with his friends. 'I have got so fed up with it on the conference circuit,' he said. 'It is expected that you will spend the evenings drinking, and it is hard to find people who don't drink to talk to.' Theological colleges often have a strong drinking culture.

- **Stress, anxiety or suppressed anger or guilt:** when an addict seeks help, it may be for anything but the addiction, since this is the thing that she or he sees as necessary to their survival. For example, Elaine had always been driven to succeed and was deeply hurt by even the slightest criticism. She would bury her anger for weeks or months, and then a drinking bout would release it all in one go. It was only when her partner insisted that they go for relationship counselling that she began to make the connection between her life story, her drinking and the explosive anger.

- **Learned behaviour**, especially growing up with addicts of one kind or another. If you grow up in a household where there is heavy drinking, it can be difficult to understand that this is abnormal or get an objective sense of your own drinking habits. Rona's father was a priest, and he and her mother drank every day at lunchtime and in the evening. When her father went on retreat for a few days, her mother would always pack his suitcase and include a half bottle of whisky. When there was strain on the family budget, her parents would switch to cheaper alcohol but never cut it out. It was years before Rona realized that their drinking pattern was unusual, or that although she herself did not drink at lunchtime, because she did drink every evening, she was heading towards a dependency on alcohol.

- **Lack of care and nurture in the early years.** Ideally as babies or small children we go through cycles of need and satisfaction, emotionally and physically. As we have seen in discussing attachment, if they are well enough met, without smothering, we can build up a reasonable expectation that while we might become hungry or lonely or uncomfortable, sooner or later someone will take that seriously and do something about it. We also learn self-reliance to see us through the gaps, and such 'good enough' experience helps us to develop a sense of self that is confident and creative. Without it, the inner landscape of the developing child may become very bleak indeed. Instead of a secure connection with the cycles of life there is an ongoing, overwhelming emptiness which cannot be filled.

Addiction and the family

There is only one real deprivation, I decided this morning, and that is not to be able to give one's gift to those one loves most . . . The gift turned inward, unable to be given, becomes a heavy burden, even sometimes a kind of poison. It is as though the flow of life were backed up.[6]

An addict never exists in isolation. Anyone who is in contact with him or her is affected: partners, children, work colleagues, friends, neighbours. It may be obvious to them that the addict is being destroyed by alcohol, little yellow pills or a cycle of destructive relationships, but as far as the addict is concerned this is their very lifeblood. This is why the hallmark of addiction is denial. Before a person can address their addiction, they have to question the very thing they rely on.

Anyone close to an addict, then, easily finds they are caught up in denial, leading to a system of what is known as co-dependency, all designed to keep the addict and the object of the addiction together. Co-dependency means behaving in such a way that the other person is enabled to carry on being the way they are. It is the downside of being easy-going – when what addicts actually need is tough love. The kind of pattern that occurs very often when a family is caught up in addiction is shown in the table on page 174 (these roles can of course be substituted by friends, etc.).

---

6 May Sarton, 1973, *Journal of a Solitude*, London: Norton Paperbacks.

The addict . . .	The spouse/ partner . . .	The children . . .	The colleagues (including, all-too often, doctors and pastors) . . .
Denies the problem	Covers up	Cover up	Cover up
Blames others	Makes excuses	Make excuses	Accept excuses
Gets angry when criticized	Does two people's work in the home	Learn to swallow their feelings	Refuse to confront; don't want to look at their own habits
Spends family money on alcohol/drugs/ gambling, etc.	Takes on extra work to shore up the finances	Overachieve or underachieve	Fail to question
Becomes unpredictable/ depressed/ violent	Works harder outside the home in order to ignore what is going on inside	Stop bringing friends home; stay away from home; try to calm/soothe/ make everything all right	Stay away
Loses trust	Swallows own feelings	Worry about parents and try to look after them	Bring jobs, responsibilities to an end
Despairs, becomes depressed	Feels shame, isolation	Feel shame, isolation, confusion	Keep their distance
Begins to have physical problems	May use alcohol or anti-depressants, etc., in order to cope	May start using alcohol/drugs. May fall into damaging relationships	
Suffers from the addiction	Suffers from the addiction	Suffer from the addiction	Suffer from the addiction

Children of alcoholics or other addicts usually suffer from some or all of the following:

- violence, abuse, family rows,
- conflict between love and anger,
- fear of intimacy,
- fear of their own anger,
- shame,
- having to guess what is normal and/or acceptable in family life,
- a sense of competition with a lover who always wins,
- difficulty in expressing feelings (especially when the mother is the addict) in case, for example, expressing feelings sets off a bout of drinking,
- ambivalence about the sober parent, who may be the 'safe' parent but who still fails to protect the children and may make impossible demands.

How can you help?

The first and greatest problem is admitting there is a problem. On the other hand, confronting the problem head on will usually meet with a blank denial, so often there is little you can do except watch out for a crisis that may turn out to be an opportunity: a drunk driving charge, a relationship breaking up, losing a job, a sudden deterioration in health or an approach from a family member seeking help. Usually the GP is the first person to approach or Alcoholics Anonymous, Narcotics Anonymous or some other specialist organization or rehab centre. There are some things you can do yourself, however,

- **Be aware of danger signals** – in yourself, in colleagues, in people for whom you have pastoral responsibility. In alcohol addiction the following apply (most of which are transferrable to other addictions):
  - Tolerance: an increase in the amount needed to achieve the desired effect – or a noticeable diminished effect with the same amount of alcohol,

- Withdrawal symptoms: shaking, sweating, stomach upsets, using tranquillizers or other drugs to cope with the lack of alcohol,
- persistent failed attempts to control or cut down on drinking,
- getting angry with anyone who suggests you might have a problem,
- preoccupation with obtaining and maintaining supplies of alcohol,
- giving up other activities in favour of drinking,
- isolating yourself,
- continuing to drink despite obvious health problems,
- legal problems caused by drinking,
- relationship problems,
- failure to keep appointments, fulfil work tasks, look after children, etc.,
- repeated accidents, falling over, etc.

- **Never argue with a drunk.** A person under the influence of drink or drugs will not be able to engage in rational argument. They may seem to be having a conversation with you, but the next day they will usually have forgotten all about it. Do not waste time having long, sentimental conversations. If necessary, make it clear that you do not talk to them in this state, but are happy to talk at some other time.
- **Exercise tough love.** Colluding with addiction only makes it worse and being prepared to be hated may be the most useful thing you can do. Doug had been in therapy for two years, and his therapist suspected he had an alcohol problem, though he never admitted to it. The first time he turned up to his ten a.m. session drunk, she refused to see him. The second time, she put him in her car and drove him to his GP surgery. The GP referred him to AA, and from there he became sober. Nevertheless, he said that if he had had a gun with him that day, he would have shot his therapist.
- **Support family and friends in naming their problems.** For example, Ashley's mother was in the advanced stages of alcoholism. Ashley was constantly getting critical phone

calls from members of her mother's church community wanting to know why she did not do more to care for her mother and did not feel able to say what her mother's problem was and why she was unable to help. Eventually someone rang who did not criticize Ashley, but after making a few enquiries, asked outright, 'Does your mother have a problem with alcohol?' Ashley was flooded with relief that someone had recognized what was going on and how helpless she was in this situation, and this empowered her to be able to name the problem to others. She did not always get a sympathetic response, but she was able to fend off the criticism, and build an understanding with others of what the real problem was.

- **Support recovering addicts in saying no.** When it comes to a common addiction like alcohol, one of the greatest enemies of recovery is people who find it hard to accept that this matters. Some people even find it an exciting challenge to draw the recovering alcoholic back into the drinking fold. To have an ally who understands that it is important to say no can be of enormous help on social occasions, as can practising saying it with a trusted other. You might even be able to help a person to find ways of phrasing a refusal that are hard to argue with, such as specific health reasons, for example heart trouble or diabetes.

- **Respect confidentiality** – of the addict and the family members. Alcoholics Anonymous and Narcotics Anonymous are Anonymous for a good reason: social pressure to go back to the old habit. For family members, the addiction can be a great source of shame and vulnerability: respect any confidences. It may be appropriate to recommend Al-Anon, which exists for relatives of alcoholics, and is also an anonymous organization.

Finally, there is a continuing argument among health professionals as to whether addiction is a choice or a disease. It can be very distressing for family members when they have gone through the trauma of a person being hospitalized for alcohol or drug abuse to be told that the hospital has no responsibility in relation to their addiction: it is a choice, not an illness. Doctors themselves are divided over this, and feelings can run high. You may not be able to influence medical opinion, but do be prepared to talk through these issues with the people involved.

12

Eating Disorder

Eating disorder is a form of mental ill health in which the body suffers directly from the ills of mind and spirit. We do not know why some people are more susceptible than others, though it is possible to trace some associated patterns. It does seem that in general people are divided between those who instinctively understand – and possibly suffer from some form of – eating disorder and those who are blessed with a constitution – and relationship to food – that makes it simply incomprehensible. If you fall into the latter group it is important to spend some time understanding what eating disorder is and what its effects might be.

Eating disorders are very much a disease of our time, and were only really recognized and defined in the 1980s. Although they still affect women more than men, the number of men presenting with eating disorders is increasing, as is the number of young children, aged ten or even less.

In their extreme forms eating disorders develop in two ways:

- Anorexia nervosa.
- Bulimia nervosa.

Compulsive eating and obesity are also on the increase. Certain kinds of obesity are closely associated with poverty – not only because of the kind of food available on a low budget, media pressure to eat certain kinds of food and poor educational resources, but because food is about far more than simply nutrition itself.

Anorexia nervosa

Anorexia is the so-called 'slimmer's disease'. What starts as a diet becomes an obsession and is often accompanied by intense exercise, so that not only is there insufficient food, but the body's resources are used to the limit. Weight drops to below what is normal or healthy: a person is officially anorexic once they are more than 25 per cent below the minimum ideal weight. Once it has set in, anorexia seems to have its own dynamic that takes over, moving on from dieting to starvation.

Table 1: The progression of anorexia

In the early stages the dieter may get high on fasting and exercise (itself a potentially addictive activity because of the good feeling from endorphins released into the body); later, depression becomes more dominant. Being underweight over a long period of time begins to affect concentration and mood and can lead to difficulty in taking much interest in other things apart from maintaining a low weight.

We have seen how addiction brooks no competition, and anorexia resembles addiction in its obsessive single-mindedness. Lynette, a talented actor, had severe anorexia throughout her teens. She sees it as a decision she made when she was 14: 'I knew I had to do something, and I became close to becoming a heroin addict. I chose anorexia, because I thought I had a better chance of surviving.' This may have been true, but nevertheless, anorexia is highly self-destructive and very difficult to dislodge. Instead of being dependent on a substance like alcohol or heroin, the anorexic becomes dependent on food refusal.

Someone in the grip of anorexia defends their low weight with all their resources: lying about what they eat, hiding food, wearing loose clothes to disguise how thin they are. At the same time, their whole identity is tied up with being thin and letting go of that to the slightest extent is simply terrifying. Perhaps because of this, a marked feature of anorexia is a distortion of body image: it is too threatening to recognize that you are not only slim but dangerously thin. The body may be dramatically underweight but the anorexic person will still look in the mirror and see themselves as fat.

Although they themselves avoid eating, most anorexics are intensely interested in food and may even work in the food industry or in cafes and restaurants where they are in a position to feed others. People living with anorexics may find themselves wanting to eat more than usual, somehow picking up the anorexic's split-off desire for food: this desire is so deeply buried that it is unconsciously projected on to others, as described in Chapter 2.

If anorexia goes untreated for a long time, the physiological effects of extreme underweight begin to set in and some may affect an anorexic person for the rest of their life. These are the same as in any situation where a person does not have enough to eat:

- weakening of the heart,
- muscle wasting and ligament damage,
- slowing down of the gut – which enables a person to get by on less food without feeling hunger pangs,
- bone density loss, making the anorexic vulnerable to osteoporosis and fractures,
- menstrual periods stopping or failing to start,
- loss of sexual function and desire,
- hair loss or the development of downy hair on the body (perhaps to protect the body from the effects of underweight),
- problems with sleeping,
- difficulties with temperature regulation, especially feeling cold.

Although some people do recover from anorexia, for many it becomes a lifelong problem. They may develop strategies for maintaining a reasonable body weight, but will always be at risk at times of particular stress, when a reversion to anorexia will be the first port of call.

For example, Penny was in and out of hospital for most of her teens with anorexia. The ligaments in her feet are damaged by the disease, so she permanently has to use orthotics, and this prevented her from becoming a dancer, something she very much wanted to do. At 30, she manages to maintain a low body weight just within normal range, has married and has children. Pregnancy and the weight gain involved were extremely stressful for her, but she came through. She still eats quite differently from her husband and worries that her daughters will pick up her own habits. Her paid work is cooking for a cafe for whom she provides delicious cakes. When Penny is under stress, she is tempted to let her weight fall, but she knows that in her teens she nearly died from anorexia and that she has to stay alive for her family. So far she has managed to stay just on the right side of anorexia, but it is a constant struggle. For her, two squares of chocolate can represent a major loss of control.

Toni, a writer, began to suffer from anorexia while she was at university back in the 1950s, before it was recognized as a disease. She has since realized what it was, but at the time neither she nor anyone else understood that she needed treatment. She is still extremely thin, and at times of stress, her body weight tends to fall below what it should be. At 70, she was diagnosed with osteoporosis, a common side effect of anorexia: critical bone development in adolescence is affected and in some people bone density never returns to normal. This is distressing in itself, but especially so since she blames herself: a lifetime of depriving herself has contributed to the osteoporosis, and she has not even benefited from the enjoyment she might have had from food if she had not had anorexia.

There is no doubt that anorexia is a life-threatening disease, and the sufferer may require a spell – or spells – in hospital to get their weight to a point where they can begin to work on the problem. This stage of treatment can be very distressing for the patient and those close to him or her. By the patient, the necessary weight gain can be experienced as an abuse of their very sense of self, while for everyone else it is the weight loss that is the abuse. On discharge, the entire family's eating habits may be dominated by the need to maintain a manageable level of food intake for the anorexic member – a process that can become exasperating, cause conflict with siblings, and sometimes seem thankless.

The majority of anorexics (around 75 per cent) do recover in terms of being able to maintain an acceptable weight, but the outlook is less good in terms of becoming comfortable with their own body image, letting go a preoccupation with food, and being able to maintain intimate relationships. In extreme cases, of course, it can lead to death, and this may be experienced by family and friends as a prolonged and agonizing suicide.

Clare Park, a photographer who suffered from anorexia, has produced powerful and disturbing images of how the anorexic experiences her body.[1] She also suggests – as do many psychologists – that there is a link between anorexia and certain personality types:

> In my experience, people blocked into the anorexic pattern of thinking are people who struggle with quite intellectual thought processes but are unable to fit them into their real life and family scenario, so they struggle with individual concepts outside their immediate control. They are often free thinkers, very individual, but also very driven and self-disciplined and with an ability to throw themselves into something. You can recover from an eating disorder, but you can't recover from the personality that helped cause the eating disorder. That vulnerability will always be there, but can be rechannelled.[2]

Bulimia

Bulimia is a different illness from anorexia but related to it: up to half of anorexics also suffer from bulimia at some point, though many people are bulimic without ever becoming anorexic. It is harder to tell how many people actually suffer from bulimia, because it is much easier to disguise than anorexia: weight may fluctuate or be steady, but a sufferer is in general more likely to be overweight than underweight.

Bulimia is the 'bingeing and vomiting' disease. While anorexics will take laxatives or vomit deliberately to get rid of food they have not been able to avoid eating, in bulimia it is vomiting, not food

---

1 See Clare Park's website, www.clarepark.tv/selfz/frame.htm
2 Clare Park in interview with Maureen Rice, 'Still at War with Our Bodies', *Observer*, 1 February 2004.

refusal, that is the addictive habit. Bulimia usually begins in adolescence and can continue well into middle age. Its main features are:

- Preoccupation with food.
- Shame and secretiveness. Before a binge the person may go to several different shops to buy food, because they are afraid that someone might notice how much food they are buying.
- Cycles of bulimic behaviour. Twice a week is a normal pattern for induced vomiting, but the illness may disappear for weeks or months at a time, recurring in times of stress.
- Physical problems, especially with the teeth and gums which can be affected by acid in the vomit. In extreme cases, there can be internal damage such as rupture of the oesophagus from prolonged and repeated straining.

Some family patterns in eating disorder

In spite of the known prevalence and seriousness of eating disorder, the cultural pressure to be thin continues and increases, alongside a worrying increase in obesity in the surrounding society. It is not surprising that many people fall prey to eating disorder, but there are also family patterns that can make them particularly vulnerable.

Eating disorder involves both the psychology of appetite and desire (feeding, biting, chewing) and self-image, body shape becoming the main means of being acceptable. If human beings consist of body, mind and spirit, eating disorder is a flight into body: all psychological and spiritual dis-ease becomes concentrated there, and as with all mental health problems the sufferer may also be acting out the unacknowledged difficulties in the body of the family.

Anorexia and bulimia have different profiles. Whereas people with anorexia are often high achievers and somewhat driven, bulimia may be associated with lower levels of achievement and with buried shame and/or anger. Either form of eating disorder may be a desperate attempt to control the uncontrollable.

The family therapist Salvador Minuchin approaches anorexia as a family matter. Anorexia may be an attempted solution by an individual – or an individual solution used by the family to face the underlying dysfunction.[3]

In the body of the anorexic's family, we may find a generalized anxiety about sexual identity. The body of an anorexic is at risk not only of starvation but of losing its capacity to reproduce, and anorexia often involves a crisis in sexual identity, which may be reflected in the underlying anxieties of the parents. Mothers of anorexic children are often gifted and energetic but may be ambivalent about their roles as women, particularly in a generation where they gave up careers or other ambitions in order to have children. Likewise a father may have difficulty in coming to terms with his children becoming sexual beings in adolescence and push them away from what was previously a close and loving relationship. The child reacts by behaving in such a way that she or he remains in a child's body.

Other family characteristics that incline people to anorexia include:

- unresolved conflict that is never discussed,
- over-involvement as a family, sometimes known as 'enmeshment', which does not allow for adolescents to separate successfully from the family,
- a rigid approach to life and high expectation of achievement.

Sometimes, the conflict gets played out in excessive dieting leading to crisis and eventually outside intervention. Unfortunately food and eating – the symptom – can then become the focus of the family problems, and the original problem continues to be ignored. Starving yourself demands a lot of attention and – like any suicide threat – can be a way of expressing anger that cannot otherwise be expressed.

It is easy for the identification of family patterns to sound pejorative, but families do not create them on purpose. For example, Wanda and Kenneth had both started successful careers, and when they married they intended to have a large family. It was a great shock to them when their first child was born with a genetic

---

3 Salvador Minuchin, 1974, *Families and Family Therapy*, London: Tavistock, Ch. 12.

disorder, which meant his hearing was seriously impaired. A genetic counsellor told them that any child of theirs would have a one in four chance of having this disorder, and their second child, Tamsin, was free of it. Their third child, however, suffered from the same disease as the first.

Each birth, of course, was subject to the same statistical chance as any of the others, but they had always wanted a large family and it seemed possible that a fourth child might somehow restore the balance in the family and give Tamsin a sibling who was not deaf. By the time Wanda was pregnant with her fourth child, however, Tamsin was approaching adolescence, and she was furious with her mother for risking having another deaf child. Sadly, this child also suffered from the genetic disorder.

In spite of all these problems, it was a close, loving and supportive family, and Wanda and Kenneth did their best to see that their three deaf children had all the same opportunities as Tamsin. The family worked together to overcome the problems experienced by the three children with hearing difficulties, but inevitably at some cost. It was Tamsin, the one child who was unaffected, who developed anorexia and spent most of her teens in and out of hospital. Several times she came close to starving herself to death. This was an almost unbearable time for her parents, but they did manage to support her through to a point where she was able to go away to university – as did her siblings – and maintain an acceptable weight. For them it was, as Wanda put it, 'a massive education in letting go'.

The family histories of people with bulimia – in contrast with those of anorexics – tend to be full of open conflict, and there is often a history of addiction and/or abuse somewhere in the family. The person suffering from bulimia has often had to develop a pseudo-mature self to compensate for parents who are for one reason or another unavailable, and to let go of this can feel extremely threatening. People with bulimia often have a highly functioning and caring 'false self' masking profound neediness and low self-esteem, so that their close relationships tend to become over-dependent and stormy. Like anorexia, bulimia is a self-destructive disease and hard to dislodge. It is also very easily disguised.

Any person with an eating disorder may be desperately trying to break out of a family pattern, and even before the eating disorder takes hold, families can make it very difficult for children with genuine weight problems to stick to a diet. Sometimes this is an unconscious power play on the part of family members who have their own weight problems – and it is part of the family identity to be fat. Consciously they may want the best for their children but unconsciously they will sabotage the diet: keeping a person different and therefore marginalized in the outside world prevents them from separating from the family.

This can lead to terrible conflicts within the person trying to break out, which become manageable only through an illness, which may be of some other kind altogether. Carla, for example, came from a family where everyone was fat and worried about their weight, though no one ever did anything about it. The only thin person in the family was her grandmother, who ate very little but produced huge meals for everyone else. When Carla began to lose weight, her mother worried aloud at every meal about whether she was ill or developing anorexia. If she gave up her diet and binged on cheese sandwiches, her father heaved a sigh of relief. These attitudes set up immense guilt in Carla, who began to think that if she lost weight, she would be betraying her family. In her mid-teens she developed duodenal ulcers, and this enabled her to reach a normal body weight without anyone being able to blame her for it.

Treatment

It has been found that group experience is very helpful in treating eating disorders, and treatment will usually include a programme of cognitive behavioural therapy, which may or may not go alongside more in-depth work to look at underlying issues.

People with anorexia or bulimia are helped to explore their attitudes to food, self-image and body size and shape. They may also be given assertiveness training (with the idea of learning to say what they feel or what they need rather than expressing it through food) and taught relaxation. Physical exercise and massage may also be used to heighten awareness of their own bodies.

Anorexics are encouraged to increase their food intake in a controlled environment where anxiety is kept at a manageable level. This can be hard work for the family when the patient is discharged. They have to tread a careful line between allowing the anorexic to keep control of what she eats while trying to avoid it becoming once more a total obsession.

The symbolism of food

A shared meal lies at the heart of Christian liturgy and is a powerful symbol of our participation in the body of Christ. Food is also essential to life, and therefore closely bound up with our physical and emotional lives. Every family has a particular relationship to it. Here we will touch on four aspects of food's psychological symbolism as:

- comfort,
- a way of dealing with anger,
- a means of power,
- an image of how we deal with our relationships.

Food as comfort

When we are babies, food and comfort are closely associated. We take in warm, sweet milk while being held and cuddled. Even adults can feel ravenously hungry after a good cry and feel the need of something warm and sweet to eat or drink. And many of us overeat when we are sad or depressed.

Unfortunately, rather than being used as a help in comforting a child, food is often used as a substitute for comfort. Instead of finding out what has distressed them, parents or carers may simply hand over a sweet or other treat to stop the child crying. This is not so bad if concern and a cuddle come with it, but if it is simply a way of getting rid of the problem, it sets up a sad relationship between food – especially sweet food – and distress.

Food as a way of dealing with anger

Human beings are needy, greedy and often hungry or frustrated, and many people express rage orally – that is they bite something, or grind or gnash their teeth. There is a natural relationship between the mouth and pain, anger or stress: before we had anaesthetics people undergoing operations were given something to bite on to help them endure the pain. In times of stress, anyone may feel the need for something to bite on: an apple or carrot may be sufficient for some, but others may need to stuff themselves with sweet food – or even bite their own hand or arm, or some tough object such as the telephone directory or a rug: 'chewing the carpet' has made its way into ordinary language to describe rage or frustration.

In overeating, a person may be quite literally swallowing their anger. There can be a lot of rage in bingeing: taking in all that food along with the physical pain and discomfort that results from it, let alone the self-disgust, is a way of turning the rage back on oneself in order not to do damage to others. Binge eaters are often very caring people, and may need encouragement to express their anger instead of stuffing it down with food.

Food as power

In Western society, most people do not have to worry about whether there is going to be enough food to go around. Attitudes to waste have changed enormously since the post-war years. No longer do parents insist that children eat everything that is put in front of them, or serve up the same meal for days on end until it is eaten.

Yet the way children behave with food is still one of the greatest challenges there is to parental authority. It is also a way in which they express their autonomy: children now make consumer choices even before they can speak, pointing out their favourite yogurts or cereals to their parents in the supermarket before it even gets as far as the table.

These days, there are many families who do not sit down to eat together every day, and battles over food are fought at all sorts of times and in all sorts of places. When there are family meals, the dinner table may be the only place where family members come together – and can also be a platform for power play, for example:

- Children refuse to sit down with the others, or build small fortresses around their place with cereal packets or whatever is available.
- Daughters assert their slimness, sexuality and self-control over or against their mothers.
- Mothers try to persuade sons they will never be strong and manly without their food – or that no one will ever be able to provide for them as she does.

- Siblings vie with each other for who has the most or the best of the food (and therefore affection).
- Food is rejected, criticized or praised, allowed to spoil, pushed on people who do not want it.
- One person's diet exerts tyranny over everyone else's meal – or those who are eating are made to feel greedy by comparison with the person who is not.

Food as an image of how we deal with our relationships

How we ourselves relate to food can be an image of how we relate to other people. The bodily habit reflects what is going on emotionally – and perhaps spiritually. On the assumption that what affects people in the community also affects those responsible for pastoral care, it is worth considering whether there are parallels between how you relate to food and how you relate to people:

- Do I know when I have had enough – or keep on eating until there is nothing left? (Can I keep a balance of togetherness and separateness in a relationship?)
- Do I avoid food (people), control my intake (interaction), hold back from enjoying food (intimacy)?
- Do I nibble and pick without ever sitting down to a relaxed meal – or a deep conversation?
- Do I time my meals to fit in with other people, or eat just when I feel like it without noticing what might suit those around me?
- Am I terrified of being hungry – or of being alone?
- Do I think about food all the time – or become obsessed with the people that matter to me?
- Do I have a constant underlying sense of deprivation – in relation to food or relationships?
- Am I afraid that if I start to eat without controlling myself I won't be able to stop – or that if I get close to someone I will swallow them up or be swallowed?

The pastoral response

When an eating disorder has taken hold, there is probably little you can do to help directly, except possibly persuade the person concerned and their family to seek professional help.

The prevalence of anorexia generates immense anxiety among the parents of teenagers who fear anorexia will set in if their child decides to lose weight, but of course this can often be a healthy rather than a neurotic decision. It can be helpful to know what to look out for as danger signals:

- weight loss to below a normal range without any let up in diet and exercise,
- obsession with food,
- producing large meals and sweet things for other people to eat without sharing them,
- lying about what you have eaten,
- avoiding family meals or toying with food,
- disappearing to the bathroom immediately after meals,
- denial that there is any problem,
- a distorted body image,
- zealous behaviour around fasting periods in the Church's year.

Another danger signal is when the diet has been triggered by something that threatens a child or adolescent's sense of identity such as:

- parents divorcing,
- living away from home for the first time,
- a sexual experience,
- failing important exams,
- a major loss or bereavement,
- the break-up of a relationship.

As the psychoanalyst Hilda Bruch pointed out, by the 1980s anorexia was no longer an individual but a social disease, bolstered by general attitudes in Western society.[4] In a pastoral role, it may be possible to encourage discussion of attitudes to body size in various groups, and it is important to examine your own.

---

4 R. A. Gordon, 2000, *Eating Disorder: Anatomy of a Social Epidemic*, Oxford: Blackwell, p. 92. See also Bruch's own book, 1978, *The Golden Cage*, New Haven: Harvard University Press.

It often seems that we allow intolerance of size in a way that we would find preposterous if the same attitudes were applied to race or colour, and these cultural attitudes become internalized in the destructive patterns of eating disorder.

In a society where food is plentiful, food easily becomes divorced from nourishment. Rather it can be something to avoid, or an indulgence associated with guilt rather than satisfaction or enjoyment. Eating disorders abuse the body and divorce it from mind and spirit: greed, need, pain, misery and rage are all turned against it in a reversal of our natural relationship with food. No one would wish this on themselves: it arises from unresolved pain, guilt and self-hatred.

13

Schizophrenia and Other
Psychotic Disorders

In Chapter 9, we distinguished between neurotic and psychotic illness. Schizophrenia is one form of psychotic illness, but psychosis can have other causes such as:

- major depression or bipolar disorder,
- post-traumatic stress syndrome,
- current stress/burn out,
- use of hard drugs,
- advanced dementia.

In this chapter we will look in some detail at schizophrenia itself and how it may appear in the church community, before returning to pastoral issues in psychosis generally.

Schizophrenia
Around one in a hundred people is diagnosed with schizophrenia at some point in their life. It may be a lifelong problem or an episode from which a person recovers – especially in late adolescence or in old age.

A diagnosis of schizophrenia can be very frightening both for the patient and for friends and relatives, and reactions are not helped by the horror film image of the 'split personality', or the common use of 'schizophrenic' to describe being in two minds about something. The associations arise because schizophrenia does involve massive mood swings as well as thought disorder, hearing voices and not being sure what are your thoughts and feelings and what are other people's.

Not much is known about the causes of schizophrenia, though there is probably a genetic component. Stress and socio-economic factors, as well as the use of hard drugs, may contribute to onset and relapse. It can be terrible for parents who find their late adolescent or early adult child is diagnosed with schizophrenia, not only because of the implications for their child's life, but also because they will inevitably wonder if they are to blame. It is important to remember that schizophrenia often occurs in families that most people would think of as 'good enough' and does not occur particularly often in depriving and violent families.

Symptoms of schizophrenia

Schizophrenia is not simply one illness but a set of symptoms. One of the most alarming symptoms for friends and family is extreme mood swings. Someone who is usually kind, gentle and loving suddenly becomes violent and difficult. When the illness begins, there may be a slow, insidious but generalized change of personality over around two years, or a sudden onset, often after a series of stressful events. The person seems to develop a different relation to reality – perhaps the closest we can get to it is to imagine living out some of our dreams and nightmares in our waking life. Symptoms fall into three main categories:

- **Delusions:** these are fixed beliefs that cannot be shifted by appeal to reason or facts. So-called delusions of grandeur are common: believing that you are Jesus or royalty or some important cultural figure. People with schizophrenia also often believe that they are being persecuted in some way, and this is what is meant by paranoid schizophrenia.
- **Ideas of reference:** delusions are often associated with 'ideas of reference'. This means reading a personal significance into unrelated events – something we all do to some extent. For example, if it is really important to get somewhere on time and your train is cancelled, and there is a traffic jam on the road route you can begin to feel that all

this is a conspiracy against you. For schizophrenics, such feelings can become realities in their minds.

- **Hallucinations and changes in perception:** seeing, hearing, smelling or tasting things that are not there. Auditory hallucinations include hearing voices that seem to speak out loud inside one's head. They may tell you to do things, or comment endlessly – and negatively – on what you are doing. People may seem to be speaking to themselves when they talk back to the voices, or laugh or shout. The voices become dangerous if they tell you to kill yourself or damage someone else. Visual hallucinations mean you see things that are not there, or see them move when they are still. Hallucinations of smell and taste may be associated with a fear that you are being poisoned.

- **Thought disorder:** this may begin with poor concentration, and develop into odd associations, speaking in verse or 'word salads' where the language has no structure. Sometimes the apparent nonsense hints at something a person would like to express but cannot, and someone who knows or gets to know them well may be able to interpret. In *Hamlet*, Ophelia appears to suffer from thought disorder in the extremity of her grief after Hamlet, her beloved, kills her father. The description of her by one of the gentlemen of the court shows how disordered speech of this kind can carry seeds of rational discourse:

[Ophelia] . . . speaks things in doubt
That carry but half sense. Her speech is nothing,
Yet the unshaped use of it doth move
The hearers to collection; they yawn at it,
And botch the words up to fit their own thoughts,
Which, as her winks and nods and gestures yield them,
Indeed would make one think there might be thought,
Though nothing sure, yet much unhappily.[1]

---

1 *Hamlet*, Act IV, scene 5.

Thought disorder can also mean being uncertain as to what are your own thoughts and what are someone else's, in three different ways:

- **Thought insertion,** when someone else's thoughts seem to come and take over your head and use your mind as a place to think them.
- **Thought broadcast,** when it seems as though your thoughts must be being heard by everyone else.
- **Thought withdrawal,** when it is as though your thoughts are being stolen – even sucked out of your brain as though by a vacuum cleaner.

Other symptoms can include inappropriate emotional reactions which can be disconcerting to other people and physical symptoms such as weight loss, digestive problems, restlessness, and unusual physical strength.

Treatment
Research has shown that the most effective treatment for schizophrenia is a combination of drugs and some form of psychotherapy, but not everyone is able to access both of these.

Drugs
Drugs remain the main treatment for schizophrenia, and may be taken as tablets, by injection or in a syrup. Sometimes these are long-acting drugs with effects lasting up to a month. It is important to keep the dosage as low as possible because of side effects, but often one of the biggest problems is persuading the person with schizophrenia to take the drugs regularly. This can be extremely frustrating for friends and family or the surrounding community.

There are two main reasons why people stop taking the drugs:

- Side effects, which may include drowsiness, depression, nightmares, impotence, blurred vision, weight gain and something known as 'tardive dyskinesia' – involuntary movements such as sucking your lips, moving your jaw from side to side, eyebrow twitching, shrugging your shoulders and also swallowing difficulties.

- Believing that the symptoms are not an illness but realities in the outside world. This is very hard to deal with as the person feels they are being cut off from reality by the drugs, and may have a real sense of being violated by them – or by anyone who tries to persuade them to seek treatment.

Psychotherapy

Where in-depth psychotherapy is successful it is usually very intense and long term, but it is not usually considered the most effective treatment – partly because of the resources required for it to take place.

On the other hand, supportive, cognitive-based therapy is often very helpful in enabling a person to stay in the community. For people with schizophrenia, ordinary daily living – cooking, self-care and so on – can be hard, and rehab, which teaches people strategies for these, can help.

For hospital outpatients, supportive group therapy combined with drugs has been found to be more effective than drug treatment alone, especially when it focuses on life plans, problems and relationships and practical questions around work and daily living. It also helps reduce isolation, which is a major problem with this illness, and retain contact with the ordinary world.

Family therapy also significantly reduces relapse rates during the first year after a time in hospital. Again this is usually done on a strategic, problem-solving basis. Families are encouraged to establish a daily routine and also, when a problem arises, to convene a family meeting to identify just what the problem is and work out possible solutions.

A large number of people do learn to live with their voices, using strategies for filtering them out or ignoring them, such as walking into another room or making some sort of diversion like coughing or sneezing when they start up. Some people simply talk back or tell them to go away.

Hospital or prison?

With the ever-increasing squeeze on the NHS many people with schizophrenia end up in prison rather than hospital. Prisoners were interviewed in a recent survey by the Office for National Statistics, and it was found that 14 per cent of all the women,

10 per cent of the men on remand and 7 per cent of the sentenced men had been assessed within the previous year as having a functional psychosis (schizophrenia or bipolar disorder). These rates are much higher than for the general population, where the figure is only 0.4 per cent.

These high rates of psychosis among prisoners are also confirmed by mental health in-reach teams. A survey of clinical records of prisoners treated by them showed that 18 per cent had a diagnosis of schizophrenia, and another 18 per cent had a diagnosis of some form of psychosis at some time in their lives.[2]

Schizophrenia in the church community

Church communities often draw in people with schizophrenia, providing shelter, companionship and care. Often those who suffer from the illness inspire particular affection even though the illness itself can be the source of crisis and anxiety.

If a member of your community is tempted to take a person with schizophrenia into their home, do talk over with them what the implications might be, especially for the rest of the family, and make sure they are at the very least equipped with phone numbers for the local psychiatric services. You will often find that the person is known to the local services, and they may be able to arrange for a visit from a community nurse or volunteer or tell you the name of the consultant involved.

The liturgy of the Church can itself be an important refuge and containment. For example, Brendan is a single man in his thirties who has lived with schizophrenia since its onset in his late teens. Most of the time he manages to get by with the help of drugs and cognitive techniques, though he does occasionally need an admission to hospital to stabilize his condition.

Every Sunday morning he makes a point of going to church and occasionally he also goes to coffee afterwards. In church and in the parish hall, he sits quietly in a corner and does not like to be approached. The liturgy and, sometimes, the coffee time provide spaces where he can simply be: part of something certainly, but

---

2 Figures from MIND, mental health charity: www.mind.org.uk

not expected to be proactive. This is a situation where the going-on-being of the church is valuable in itself.

Many schizophrenics find it hard to settle anywhere: the illness makes it too difficult. It may be that a church community can provide a temporary containment, but is unable to sustain this long term. It can be very distressing when someone simply disappears and no one knows what has happened to them.

For example, a young woman, Lavinia, appeared in the congregation of a suburban church and quickly made friends. She was warm, intelligent, engaging and helpful, and everyone liked her.

After some months, however, Lavinia began to change: she appeared depressed and gradually became more and more unreliable. She lost her job as a hospital secretary and seemed increasingly isolated and confused. She began taking people aside and talking about people she had known in the past who were persecuting her and who had become voices in her head. She had to move out of the room she rented, because her landlord was being 'difficult'.

Eventually Lavinia had to be sectioned, and for the next few years she was in and out of hospital: each time her symptoms were a little bit worse, and her recovery less effective: those who were trying to care for her felt that they were fighting a losing battle with something that had Lavinia in its grip and would not let her go. Finally, she simply disappeared and this left a residue of guilt and sadness in the community. Perhaps the church community could be said to have been companions on the way, even if she was not able to make use of this for more than a few years.

This, of course, is not always the case: church communities can and do provide containment for many people with severe mental health problems – and find their lives significantly enriched in return.

Some pastoral issues in relation to psychosis in general

Pastoral involvement with anyone who has a psychotic illness can be very taxing because feelings run high: people may become fearful and/or angry when confronted with psychosis. The most difficult thing can be 'to keep your head when all about you are losing theirs and blaming it on you',[3] as well as to accept that you

---

3 As in Rudyard Kipling's 'If'.

may be rejected or perceived as an enemy by the very person you are trying to help.

You may well find yourself pulled apart between the different people affected by the illness: the sufferer, the family and your own community. Sometimes – particularly when there is a new onset of psychosis – the biggest hurdle can be acknowledging there is a problem before something extreme happens such as a violent outburst, suicide attempt or a person going missing. Psychotic episodes usually require psychiatric intervention at some stage, and may involve the possibility of sectioning under the Mental Health Act, so it is worth knowing what that involves.

Sectioning under the Mental Health Act

A person who is 'sectioned' is detained in hospital whether they are willing or not. In order for this to happen, usually three people are required:

- a mental health professional (such as a counsellor or community nurse) or close relative,
- a specially trained doctor,
- a registered medical practitioner (such as the GP or a duty doctor from the hospital).

If at all possible at least one of the doctors should know the patient personally.

There are two reasons for sectioning someone:

- either they urgently need treatment,
- or it is necessary for their own safety or that of other people. For example, the voices may be urging them to commit suicide, or they may have paranoid delusions which may cause them to be violent to someone else.

Sometimes, of course, both these reasons apply.

The idea of sectioning may be frightening for the patient and the family, but sometimes removal into hospital is the best – or only – thing. The police may be needed to restrain the person: they are trained in liaising with the psychiatric services when sectioning is necessary. They, as well as the psychiatric services, can be seen as heavy-handed and punitive – no one likes to see a person they love restrained against their will – though in my own experience, they generally handle these occasions sensitively, even if they have to insist. A pastoral worker who is present while all this takes place may be able to hold some common sense ground between fear and anger.

Once a person is in hospital, you may also be able to help the patient and the family discuss treatment – the dosage level of drugs for example – with the professionals. If there is a local patient advocacy scheme, do make sure they are involved as they are extremely useful for this and know their way around the system.

As always, it is important to maintain good contacts where possible with local doctors and hospitals and to have someone you can ask for advice. It is also worth finding out about your local mental health advocacy scheme and/or branch of MIND so that you can ensure the patient and/or family are in touch with them.

Caring for the family

Living with someone whose view of the world is badly damaged places a constant strain on one's sense of self. The consequences of mental illness can feel extremely rejecting for family or friends. In addition, they often experience a sense of being hostage to the illness. Time and again work or social arrangements have to be broken or reorganized, because a crisis has occurred. This in itself is highly stressful, and the family may also face ongoing difficulties in dealing with the professionals: the system itself is under great strain, however well-intentioned the people who work within it. Someone who can allow family or friends to ventilate their anger and exasperation while accepting that this is still a loving relationship can help them sustain their sense of their own sanity.

One major problem that sometimes arises is when the family or community believe a person needs sectioning and the doctors do not. This can be devastating – and very frightening for those involved. In its early stages, an illness may not be at all obvious to the outside world, as in a case described by Gwynneth Hemmings, one-time secretary of the Schizophrenia Association, who interviewed the wife of someone who developed schizophrenia in mid-life:

My husband gave the impression to the outside world that he was a gentle, loving, hard-working man and that I was a neurotic, crazy woman who lied about what happened in the home. I stayed with him until he lost his temper with my eldest child and tried to strangle him until the boy's face went purple and his eyes bulged . . . My husband's eyes were completely enraged and our voices . . . could not penetrate his head.[4]

What often happens, too, is that once a person is sectioned those who have been trying to get help for them are immensely relieved – only to find that well before they have had time to recover from the incidents leading up to sectioning, the patient is being released or let out for large parts of the day because drug treatment has begun to work, and keeping them against their will is not justified.

Caring for the patient

When visiting a psychotic patient in hospital, there will always be times when any intervention seems futile but a genuine attempt to understand is almost always worthwhile.

John Foskett, for many years chaplain at the Bethlem Royal and Maudsley hospitals in London, is convinced of this through his experience of being with severely ill people:

> Pastors can demonstrate their willingness to try and understand. They can refuse to compound the patient's sense of isolation by their regular visits, their readiness just to sit and wait out the worst . . . With others involved in treatment and care they can begin to see some picture of the significance of the illness: the form it takes, the kind of delusions or hallucinations and the effect upon the patient and relative.[5]

He goes on to describe a young man whose psychotic episode coincided with the news that his mother had cancer. He thought he was Jesus and believed he could cure her. As Foskett points out,

---

4 Gwynneth Hemmings, 1989, *Inside Schizophrenia*, London: Sidgewick and Jackson, p. 1.

5 John Foskett, 1984, *Meaning in Madness: The Pastor and the Mentally Ill*, London: SPCK, p. 147.

it is not wise to try to challenge the delusion while the patient is in a psychotic state, but there may come a time after the person has recovered when insights like this could be helpful in understanding what happened. For yourself, some insight into where the delusion is coming from may also help you to maintain your own compassion.

PART 4

Betrayal and Forgiveness

14

Betrayal and Forgiveness

The fourth part of this book has only one chapter – on betrayal and forgiveness. You may wonder what a book on psychology is doing introducing the idea of forgiveness: is that not the business of theologians? Well, yes, and no. It is a word that many psychologists fight shy of precisely because the churches have laden it with so many connotations of guilt and inadequacy. People who have much to forgive feel bad because they cannot manage it and often try to do too much too soon, so that the freedom that true forgiveness brings vanishes into the distance. Forgiveness is ultimately a spiritual matter, and there is no doubt that it can also be a matter of grace or gift, but it is a mistake to try and leap-frog into it without understanding the psychological mechanisms involved.

Furthermore, forgiveness is a theme that runs right through pastoral ministry. The pastoral context itself provides endless cycles of betrayal and forgiveness between members of a community, including those involved in pastoral care, who themselves betray and are betrayed and have to learn to forgive and be forgiven if they are to survive. Pastoral workers also hear innumerable stories of injury, of the guilt that goes with an inability to forgive, of anxiety about whether God can forgive and so on. For some pastors, there will also be a sacramental aspect in hearing confessions, giving absolution or engaging in prayer ministry and healing services. This sacramental aspect is important, and can often move someone along the path of forgiveness, or set the seal on the work of forgiveness – but it needs to happen within the context of understanding the work itself.

Why do betrayal and forgiveness go together?

Some injury is random: one person may hurt another but it happens out of the blue, as in a street attack. Other injuries involve betrayal, and I suggest that it is by looking at the relationship between trust and betrayal that we can really explore what forgiveness means. An injury is harder to let go where it involves a betrayal of trust – and of course even where the hurt is apparently random, it may feel as though it is God who is the betrayer.

Any ongoing relationship – with other human beings or with God – implies a degree of trust, and it is an assumption here that we can only really be betrayed where a measure of trust exists: 'It is not enemies who taunt me – I could bear that . . . but you, my equal, my companion, my familiar friend . . .' (Ps. 55.12–13).

We can distinguish between two levels of trust:

- 'Primal trust', which is unconscious and justified by the very nature of the relationship as between parents and children,
- The trust of covenant, which involves an implicit or explicit agreement or promise as, for example, in marriage.

Primal trust

Primal trust is trust that is unconscious, unquestioning: we do not even think about whether we trust the other person or not. It is the condition of Adam before the Fall, where there was no sense of division between himself and God. He is also at one with Eve, and he walks with God in the garden. This is the trust of a tiny baby just arrived in the world. Only gradually does the baby learn separateness from the mother – and indeed the mother from the baby.

Because primal trust is so fundamental, when it is betrayed this is experienced as a betrayal of one's very being. It is not a case of 'You promised . . .', but of discovering that things are not what you thought they were. What was experienced as warmth, nourishment, a safe and secure place turns out to be a separate human being with a life, thoughts, desires of his or her own: the shape of the universe changes.

This is not necessarily a bad thing if it happens within a secure enough environment: in fact it is necessary to the enlargement of consciousness and to developing self-reliance. Every one of us has to accommodate some betrayal of primal trust in order to grow up. For example, when a new sibling is born the first child finds the parents are preoccupied with someone else. Where the first child's attachment is 'good enough', the discovery that 'Mum and Dad can manage without me' has its advantages as well. It brings freedom. Where a child is not securely attached, the sense of betrayal may go very deep.

Betrayal of primal trust is not simply a matter for small children and babies, however, though early experience will influence how trust is developed and betrayal managed in later life. Primal trust is reactivated in intimate relationships, in sexual love, in caring situations: anywhere where a person is drawn without thinking into a close and trusting relationship.

Trust of covenant

By contrast, the trust of covenant is based on a conscious commitment. For example in 1 Samuel 18, David and Jonathan make a covenant together, soul bound to soul. Soon after this, Saul, Jonathan's father, becomes envious of David's success in battle: thereafter David's life is in danger from Saul's various attempts to kill him. Saul even makes use of the fact that his daughter Michal also loves David. He tells David he can marry her, but as a marriage gift he must provide a hundred Philistine foreskins – expecting David to die in the attempt. His hostility is further kindled when David returns with the required trophies, and Michal enables David to escape a further plot against him devised by her father.

Her brother Jonathan also does this, though he takes some persuading that his father is plotting against his friend. When he cannot believe this, David appeals explicitly to the covenant between them: 'Deal kindly with your servant for you have brought your servant in to a sacred covenant with you. But if there is guilt in me, kill me yourself. Why should you bring me to your father?' (1 Sam. 20.8). Jonathan replies that of course he would tell David if he thought his father was plotting against him. He discovers what is going on and does indeed help David to escape.

Both Michal and Jonathan demonstrate that the trust of marriage in the one case and friendship in the other outweigh what is owed by son or daughter to father. David's life is saved.

The trust of covenant goes beyond personal commitment. Anyone engaged in pastoral work is part of an implicit or explicit covenant of care within the church community. This involves many different levels, from an explicit document such as a child protection policy or health and safety regulations in a community building, to an implicit understanding of the values held by the community as a whole.

Even in everyday life the trust that is implicit in a network of relationships may be broken by what is experienced as betrayal by those who depend on it: there will always be times when even the most committed pastor is unavailable, on holiday, ill, tired, or preoccupied with something else. This is not only inevitable but essential if pastoral workers are to survive and members of the community are to relate together as adults. If another person feels badly let down, it is important to weigh up what they could reasonably expect from you, and whether you are able to offer that. It may be necessary to make what was implicit explicit: to map out where the boundaries of the relationship are.

When the implicit or explicit covenant of the community is broken this becomes a very serious matter for everyone, for example:

- A failure of care by someone who might have been expected to provide it,
- An abuse of one person's vulnerability by another,
- If a member of the community commits a serious crime: 'If that could happen here, what does it mean about us?',
- Ministry burnout – where the community has to come to terms with the demands it has collectively placed on someone who collapsed under the strain.

When something like this comes to light everyone in the community is in some sense implicated: people may have to ask themselves how it could have been going on unnoticed among them. They may be forced to reconsider just how trustworthy the 'community covenant' is, and what it is based on.

Betrayal as a risk in relationship

Both aspects of trust – primal trust and covenant – are part of any close relationship. We can be hurt, abused, attacked or wounded by enemies and strangers, but they cannot betray us, since betrayal implies a context of trust. So: spouse betrays spouse; parent betrays child; friend betrays friend; business partner betrays business partner – and so on. As soon as a relationship is formed, there is a risk of betraying and being betrayed.

This has to be so if this is to be a relationship of persons who can act freely. Take for example a child who is practising jumping off a wall into his father's arms. For the father to step aside and let him fall to the ground would certainly be an act of betrayal. Yet, jumping into his father's arms is only an act of trust if the father is free to do just that.

Trust, then, makes us vulnerable to infinite forms of betrayal, such as:

- I trusted you and you let me down.
- I was friendly and you rejected me.
- We made love and it did not mean anything to you.
- I confided in you and you treated it with contempt.

There are also many reasons why we ourselves betray others:

- When there is another agenda or other relationships and responsibilities requiring our attention.
- When there is danger, for example in shielding someone you know to have done something wrong. The extent to which this has happened in the churches over child abuse in recent decades is only now being revealed, but it also happens constantly on an everyday level, for example, covering up for a fellow pastor who has a serious drink problem or who is having an affair with a parishioner. This is often done in the name of keeping the peace. Christ himself said, 'I have not come to bring peace, but a sword' (Matt. 10.34): this can be the sword of the whistle-blower, who reveals how a system is keeping the truth hidden. When it is broken open it can be horribly painful, but it is

also an opportunity for the community to examine itself, and take responsibility for the assumptions and projections that allowed this to happen in the first place.

- When we have taken on something we cannot actually do, like Peter who said to Christ, 'I will lay down my life for you' (John 13.37), but a few hours later found it was too difficult even to admit that he knew him (John 18). There are many examples of this in ordinary life, as for example, when someone promises their sick mother, husband or wife, 'I will never let you go into a home' – and finds that promise cannot be kept because of long-term sleeplessness, social isolation and exhaustion. They may need considerable support to be able to forgive themselves.

- When we have taken on something whose implications we do not understand, like the disciples who slept in Gethsemane (Matt. 26.40ff). This failure to realize the enormity of the task is almost certain to be part of almost any marriage and of many pastoral relationships as well.

Betrayal as a problem and an opportunity

Betrayal fractures human relationships, at least temporarily, but if it is survived and forgiven it can deepen a relationship and lead to growth. Only when we are betrayed do we begin to understand what we rely on when we can no longer rely on ourselves. This is why, for example, counsellors and therapists pay such close attention to breaks and absences. If they can persuade the other person to identify and name the feelings of betrayal and those feelings can be accepted and survived, this can give an opportunity for change.

For some people, an experience of feeling betrayed by God introduces doubt, anger and anguish into that relationship too. For example, Edmund had served God all his life as monk, but by the time he was in his fifties he found himself to be the youngest member of his community: the community itself was diminishing steadily. He was increasingly isolated and carried a huge burden of care for his fellow monks. To his horror he became for the first time truly angry with God: 'How could you let this happen to me?' Like Job – and many other Old Testament figures – he had to come to terms with finding a deeper level of trust which could accommodate the fact that he did not understand where his life might be taking him.

Some responses to being betrayed

To be betrayed is always painful, and when it happens we have different ways of dealing with the pain. These tend to set in before there is even a chance to think about it, but once we are aware of our own patterns of response, we do have a measure of choice about how to respond in the long term. Some common patterns are as follows:

- Revenge,
- Denial,
- Cynicism,
- Self-betrayal,
- A flight into paranoia.

Revenge

Immediate revenge takes the form of an eye for an eye, pain for pain. It may be cathartic but it changes nothing. Its most likely result is counter-revenge, setting up the cycle of violence that we encounter at every level from personal relationships to global warfare.

When revenge is delayed, it can become narrow and obsessional: you are preoccupied with plotting what you would like to do to the betrayer. Or it can be displaced onto others who did not hurt you in the first place. For example, Kimberly had been going out for two years with her boyfriend when he suddenly, without warning, deserted her for someone else. It was several years before she was able to establish a new relationship, since she fell into a pattern of dropping boyfriends as soon as they showed they cared about her. Only gradually did she begin to realize she was repeating the hurt that had been done to her.

In the long run, revenge does not heal: it shrinks consciousness, though if the desire for revenge can be allowed to come into awareness without acting it out, it can be a useful safety valve.

You may think about what you might like to do, but actually choose not to do it.

Denial

Denial is a way of minimizing pain by pretending – to oneself and others – that the betrayal was not important. 'Don't worry about it – it doesn't matter.' This denial, which masks the underlying anger, may be useful as a survival mechanism, and is often needed in order to survive the initial stages. It does, however, close off the possibility of something positive happening between you and the betrayer.

Cynicism

Cynicism can take the form of adopting views or making decisions such as 'All love is a cheat' or 'I've taken enough risks in my life. I will never fall in love again.' This, too, is a protective measure, but essentially sterile.

Self-betrayal

Self-betrayal is far more dangerous and is related to 'introjection' as described in Chapter 2. You identify so much with the betrayer that you use what she or he has done against yourself. This is a key problem for children who grow up in violent or abusive families, but it also takes place on a more everyday level, as when someone is mocked for their ambition to do a particular thing and decides it was a stupid idea in the first place.

In pastoral work, it is important to be alert to being told things – not just events, but secret hopes and ambitions – that people have previously kept to themselves: 'I've always wanted to be a pub pianist' or 'I wrote a poem once . . .' These meaningful, precious things can turn to dust and ashes if not heard and respected. They may also be very fragile when first confided. For example, Adrian spoke to his parish priest about the possibility of training for the priesthood. He was horrified the next Sunday when the priest announced to the congregation with great excitement, 'We have a vocation in our midst.' Adrian felt used and betrayed, and although he did eventually go forward for ordination, it threw him into doubt for some time.

Self-betrayal turns you against your own experience so that you start acting according to someone else's values and not your own.

Julian, for example, was deeply in love with Veronica, who was a few years older than he was and more experienced: it was his first sexual relationship. He was appalled to discover one day that she was sleeping with other people besides himself – something that she did not see as a problem. 'Good sex is like good food,' she told him, 'and I like to share it with my friends.' Julian was devastated. 'I thought we had love between us, but she has made it just sex.' He decided that he, too, would live in that way and started sleeping around: this brought him no pleasure and an increasing sense of self-disgust, and eventually he was able to realize that he did not wish to live in this way.

The effect of self-betrayal as a response to betrayal by others is to prevent you from truly living as yourself, for example from:

- Getting through a stage of life: if the family requirement that you be mature and responsible leaves you no space to act out the storms of adolescence (this is particularly common where there is some form of physical or mental illness in the family or a volatile relationship between the parents that takes up all the emotional space).
- Finding the confidence to practise and nurture your talents: parents, teachers, spouses tell you you are not really up to playing an instrument, for example, or that doing so is a waste of time and you internalize this.
- Following a vocation: an experience of the church or some other institution you feel drawn to leaves you feeling that it is all corrupt, rigid or institutional, and you decide you will not be part of it.
- Looking after yourself: a common form of self-betrayal among people involved in caring for others is an inability to accept when something is simply too much. It can be easier to turn to alcohol, tranquillizers or comfort eating than to confront the fact that you are overwhelmed.

A flight into paranoia

A flight into paranoia involves a vow to protect yourself from ever being hurt again after a major betrayal. In future relationships you may become absolutist in your demands: 'If you loved me you wouldn't go out to work/spend time with other people/sleep facing the other way.' It is an attempt to exclude risk but it also tends to exclude love because it makes impossible demands and rejects compromise.

Breaking the cycle: forgiveness

All these patterns, common though they are, solve nothing. How do you do something different? In working out forgiveness, there is a paradox between separateness, allowing the other person to be themselves, and vigilance – maintaining and sustaining the relationship if possible, or letting it go if it is not. Forgiveness is not shrugging off something: rather it is an active process that involves engaging with what has happened.

There are three common temptations for someone who has been betrayed:

- To be comfortable: saying too hastily, 'I don't want any bad feeling between us' or 'I forgive you' or 'Let's be friends'.
- To be righteous. This is often unconscious and may act in subtle ways, but its basic form is to choose to 'rise above' the unpleasantness of the other and disguise this – to oneself as well – as forgiveness.
- Not to want to be bothered: 'I don't want to think about it any more.'

None of these takes on the otherness of the other person, and the third option – trying to forget – too often results in sudden surges of resentment that are hard to contain. Forgiveness is only truly meaningful not as forgetting but in terms of a wrong transformed. It is important to acknowledge that this is a long process and we may not be capable of completing it. It is here that ritual and sacrament can be immensely helpful, as long as it is remembered that they are not a magic solution.

Forgiveness involves an effort of will and carries significant risks:

- Having to go on living with the suffering: not holding on to it but letting it go while acknowledging the reality. Forgiveness is no guarantee that the betrayal will not be repeated. People are often eager that we should 'forgive and forget', but forgetting is very different from letting go, and to forgive without protecting yourself helps neither party.
- Doing without or dismantling the protective mechanisms which become part of our nature. True forgiveness may involve risking those very things that have formed our characters.
- Involving the betrayer in some kind of dialogue. If she or he denies that there is any problem it may be impossible to proceed except as an inner path, leaving the other to their own. This can be an immense problem for people who recover memories of sexual abuse in childhood. Those who abused them or who failed to protect them may deny that anything ever happened – or may be dead. The abused person is then left with the very painful task of separating themselves sufficiently to hold on to their truth without the comfort of knowing that the injury is acknowledged.
- Coming to terms with your own contribution and forgiving yourself – either for having been caught up in the cycle of violence or for colluding with it against yourself. It is here, of course, that the provisions of the church for mediating God's healing and forgiveness are very important.

Receiving forgiveness

The Lord's Prayer constantly reminds us of the relationship between forgiving and being forgiven: 'Forgive us our trespasses (or sins) as we forgive those who trespass (or sin) against us.'

Being forgiven requires being able to acknowledge our own part in something, even if there seemed to be good reasons for it at the time. This is as difficult, sometimes, as forgiving someone else. Just as there are avoidance strategies for the betrayed, there are avoidance strategies for the betrayer:

- To get caught up in a cycle of revenge. This can also lead to an expectation of being hurt or refusing to notice that the cycle has been broken by the other person.
- Denial. If you cannot acknowledge that you did something bad to the other person it is impossible to receive forgiveness. Denial can take the form of pretending nothing happened, of making excuses, of insisting that what was done was intended for the other's good. For example, if a choir director shouts at one of the singers, it may be important to acknowledge that this was bad behaviour; but in situations like this where we lose control we tend to try and justify it.

Forgiveness draws us into relationship and involves sharing the feelings and taking responsibility. This is uncomfortable for anyone. Yet, to be forgiven is required of us as well as to forgive others.

God's forgiveness

While it is important to examine the psychological processes of forgiveness closely, we cannot expect to achieve forgiveness alone. In his book *The Dance of Love*, Stephen Verney (1919–2009) points out that most cases of forgiveness in the New Testament use the Greek word *aphesis*, which means letting go in three senses:

- Releasing prisoners and slaves,
- Relaxing tension, as in a taut rope,
- Letting go horses at the beginning of a race.[1]

Forgiving does not mean that everything is all right. What it does mean is that you are becoming free of what has occurred. If we can forgive another by letting go, this is not to opt out, but to allow the separateness of the other person's path. If we can accept forgiveness we, too, are transformed.

---

1 Stephen Verney, 1989, *The Dance of Love*, London: Harper Collins.

The Benedictine monk Sebastian Moore speaks of forgiveness as a transformation of consciousness and draws a distinction between God's forgiveness and our own.

- When I forgive you, there is a transformation in me. I have relented, abandoned a stance.
- When God forgives me, I am transformed: my heart is unhardened and this originates my ability to forgive someone else.

Forgiveness, then, is not just a question of logic. To have been forgiven means to have received the transformation that it brings about – setting you free from resentment. So, argues Moore, 'divine forgiveness either creates a community or it is not received'.[2]

This sounds very reasonable, but day by day each one of us is confronted with our own inability to be loved and by betrayal. Sometimes we may be too wounded by the event or by the magnitude of the betrayal to manage forgiveness.

Forgiving the unforgivable

In his play, *The Gift of the Gorgon*, Peter Shaffer explores the question of whether there are unforgivable acts.[3] A playwright, Edward, is desperate that people should confront the true horror of violence: only then will the slate be wiped clean. He argues that sometimes revenge is right, as when Clytemnestra murdered Agamemnon in revenge for his sacrifice of their daughter.

Edward marries a woman who argues that even if she desired revenge on someone it would be wrong. She persuades him to temper his violent plays, and they become highly successful, but he resents her influence, seeing her as the Gorgon that turns him to stone.

Eventually he decides to write a horrific play about Northern Ireland, in which a woman is torturing a terrorist as a personal

2 Sebastian Moore, 1977, *The Crucified Jesus is No Stranger*, Mahwah, NJ: Paulist Press, p. 82.

3 Peter Shaffer, 1993, *The Gift of the Gorgon*, London: Penguin.

punishment for the death of her daughter: at the end she dances at his death. The play is a flop.

Shaffer's play ends with a terrible series of betrayals, Edward having sworn to make his wife believe that there are such things as unforgivable acts. At last he involves her in his own death – something she cannot forgive. She writes to his son asking him to expose what has happened, and he replies, 'You must forgive or die.' At the same time Edward's spirit comes back to demand that she takes her revenge.

The play ends with her struggling to drown out these demands with cries of 'I forgive'. It is clear that this forgiveness is an act of will that she is going to have to go on making continuously for the rest of her life.

Shaffer's play demonstrates that forgiveness is more than a matter of feeling. At the same time, we cannot always tell whether we have forgiven someone or not. Clarissa Pinkola Estes, a Jungian analyst, offers some useful guidelines for checking this out:

- The rage has gone (though not necessarily the sorrow).
- You have nothing left you want to say about it.
- You understand what was behind the person acting as they did.
- You are not bound to a desire for anything – you are free to go.[4]

These things do not happen overnight. For example, Sybil's career crashed when she had a breakdown: as she fell deeper and deeper into depression she recovered memories of a childhood rape. One of the most painful aspects of her story was the fact that her parents had known and done nothing, had even gone on relating to the man who raped her as though nothing had happened.

Twelve years after she first got in touch with what had happened to her, she was able to say that she had thoroughly processed the experience and was beginning to let go. She could not be bothered to be angry any more. She had said everything she

---

4 Clarissa Pinkola Estes, 1998, *Women who Run with the Wolves*, London: Rider, p. 373.

could possibly want to say, and she understood the environment in which this terrible thing had happened. Could she ever really be free, however, of the desire that her parents should have acted differently? Was that maybe a wound that would never leave her?

Maybe, she said, I can't really sign up to having forgiven, and I don't know that I can even if I want to, but at least I can say that there might come a time. Forgiveness, as Estes points out, is 'not a hundred per cent proposition'. 'The important thing is to begin and continue.'[5]

Summary and toolkit

Betrayal and forgiveness happen in the context of relationship. Real betrayal implies some pre-existing trust.

Trust is of two kinds:

- Primal trust: unquestioning, unconscious. Adam before the Fall.
- Trust based on word: covenant, contract, promises – implicit and explicit.

Some reasons for betraying trust are:

- Other agendas,
- Being in danger,
- Having taken on something we can't do,
- Having taken on something we don't understand.

Five possible responses to betrayal are:

- Revenge: immediate or delayed, real or fantasized. Escalates violence, shrinks consciousness.
- Denial: pretends there is no problem.
- Cynicism: avoids further trust.
- Self-betrayal: rubbishing the thing in yourself that was vulnerable.

---

5 Estes, *Women*, p. 369.

- Paranoia – protect oneself against any possibility of further betrayal. Excludes risk, and also relationship.

(A sixth possible response is, of course, to begin on the path to forgiveness.)

Three temptations for the betrayed that sidestep forgiveness

- To be comfortable (not wanting disagreement/conflict),
- To be righteous – rising above it,
- To forget.

Temptations for the betrayer

- Getting caught up in a cycle of revenge,
- Denial.

Knowing you have forgiven

- The rage has gone.
- You have nothing left you want to say about it.
- You understand why it happened.
- You are not bound by a desire for anything: you are free.

Appendix

Reflecting on Your Pastoral Practice

There is no such thing as the perfect pastoral worker (or indeed the perfect community in which to engage in pastoral activity). There is, however, such a thing as a pastoral worker who can reflect on and learn from his or her mistakes. Whether you do this alone, in prayer or with a supervisor or colleague, this can be a painful process, but it is not something to be afraid of. Just as we become physically fitter by exercising our muscles, so we can become intellectually and emotionally fitter by exercising our minds and hearts. The payoff – as with physical exercise – is that situations become easier and less threatening, and we can come to rely on our intuitions, analyses and feelings.

It is, of course, a great blessing to have a trusted supervisor or colleague who can listen and give feedback on pastoral work you are engaged in. There will always be times, however, when you are thrown back on your own resources. Learning to listen in prayer – to hear what God might be saying as well as speaking what is in our hearts – is, of course, extremely valuable. Making space to reflect alone, though daunting to begin with, is also important and can help us understand ourselves as well as others. Approached in the right way this is not an extra burden, but actually an aid to survival – or even progress.

For example, Craig, a retired clergyman needed some work done on his roof, and rang a builder to arrange for him to take a look. 'Around eight o'clock OK?' asked the builder. 'Eight a.m.?' asked Craig in alarm. The builder confirmed this. 'I'm afraid,' said Craig a touch grumpily, 'that's too early for me. Can you make it nine?' It was left that the builder would come at some point, and would ring beforehand to see if Craig was in.

That night, Craig had a dream. He was changing trains at a station and running to catch the second train, which was just leaving. He got stuck in the doors as they were closing and realized he would have to jump off the train before it left the station, to avoid being swept off by a device at the end of the platform.

The next morning he was up and dressed by eight, and asked himself why he had put off the builder. There were two problems: one was that there was now no firm arrangement and he might have let the opportunity to employ a good workman slip through his fingers. The other, and deeper, problem was that he was cross with himself. Here he was, retired, and not prepared to be available at eight a.m. for a working man with a living to make. It was not a pleasant thought, especially when he began to reflect on the dream. To him it suggested that he was not managing to 'change trains' – to make an important transition.

The transition Craig was trying to make was, of course, from ministry to retirement. When he thought about it, he realized that he had been applying to the builder a strategy he had used as a pastor: not to engage in visits or phone calls before nine, except, of course, in an emergency. As a retired person, he did not need this strategy any more. He phoned the builder, explained he had made a mistake about timing, and reinstated the appointment.

In pastoral situations we are often bombarded with requests for things that are difficult to do and also with questions that are hard to answer. Saying yes or providing the wanted answer can become a knee-jerk reaction. If you can learn to give yourself time, even by simply saying, 'I will think about that', your response is likely to be more useful in the long run. Similarly, it makes sense to find ways of asking what the other person wants – and this may mean sitting down and thinking about the question you need to ask.

A common mistake is the intrusive hospital visit when somehow the theology that tells us 'We are all one' gets distorted into a lack of respect for other people's privacy. Of course visiting the sick is extremely important and part of the gospel task, but the fact that someone is in hospital does not necessarily mean they want to be visited by just anyone. Living communities throw up dislikes as well as friendships, disputes as well as reconciliation. If you have doubts as to whether a visit from you might be welcome, do not be afraid to ring the ward – or a close friend or relative of the patient – and ask.

In the first chapter we suggested that effective pastoral intervention requires bringing together thinking, feeling and acting. Here is an exercise in thinking and feeling to help you work out what you might need to do.

Some practical suggestions for reflecting on your pastoral practice

These can be used together as a complete exercise or by selecting the parts that seem to you most useful or appealing.

Space and time
Decide how much time you need and set it aside somewhere where you will not be interrupted.

Choose your space carefully:

- Inside or outside?
- Background music or silence?
- Do you want to write down what you are thinking and feeling?
- Do you want to draw or paint, or play an instrument?
- Do you think better with something simple to do – digging, sewing, or going for a walk?

Having thought about what would work best for you, an important question is: *In my life (not in an ideal one!) what is the best way for me to achieve this space and time?*

When you have selected your space and decided on your time, be inaccessible: unplug the phone; turn off the computer.

Stillness
Centre yourself with prayer.

Remember that in any situation there will be things you can influence and things you can't. There may be a particular psalm that comes to mind or a Bible story that is asking to be read. Some people find it helpful to begin with the first few lines of the prayer used daily by members of Alcoholics Anonymous, the Serenity Prayer:

> God grant me the serenity to accept the things I cannot change, courage to change the things I can and the wisdom to know the difference.

Focus on a situation/person that concerns you

- How would I sum it up to an outsider?
- What (or who) is it that bothers me about this situation?

Place it in context: some questions are

- Who is involved in this?
- Who is affected by it?
- How did I get involved – and was it appropriate?
- Where have I met a situation like this before?
- What is the extent or what are the limits of my responsibility?
- Who else has responsibilities here?

The other people involved

- When I think about this situation who comes into focus?
- Does he/she remind me of anyone?
- How much are they really like that person?
- How do I think this person sees me?
- Is their perception accurate?
- What do I accept and reject in their image of me?

Explore your feelings

- What do I feel when I have to engage with this situation? Excited? Sad? Fearful? Angry? Anxious? Helpless? Something else?
- Sit with that feeling for a couple of minutes. It is real – you might as well know about it.

- *Explore your role*

- If this were a personal situation (i.e. not in role) would I feel differently?
- If I were not bound by my role what would I like to say?
- What can I extract from that which is compatible with my role?
- What's my particular contribution in my particular role?
- What's my particular contribution given my own story?

Invoke internal support

- Who would I like to talk to about this?
- What might she/he say?
- Who would I NOT like to talk to about this – and why?
- Are there any liturgical/biblical phrases or images that come to mind?
- Can I pray about it? What happens?
- What comes to mind from films – books – pictures – poems – music?

Ask yourself these questions

- What would I *like* to happen?
- What can I change?
- What do I have to accept?
- What help do I need?

Draw/sculpt/write something to remind you of what this situation means to you.

Write down any things you have decided you need to say or do, or people you need to contact.

End with prayer or a biblical text.

Further Reading

Readers may wish to follow up some of the texts that are referred to in the footnotes for each chapter. Some more general reading is suggested below.

Chapter 1   Pastoral Activity as Participation

Campbell, A. V., 1987, *Dictionary of Pastoral Care*, London: SPCK.

Litchfield, Kate, 2006, *Tend My Flock: Sustaining Good Practice in Pastoral Care*, Norwich: Canterbury Press.

Lynch, G. (ed.), 1999, *Clinical Counselling in Pastoral Settings*, New York and London: Routledge.

Nouwen, H. J., 1979, *The Wounded Healer*, New York: Image & Doubleday.

Rose, J., 2002, *Sharing Spaces? Prayer and the Counselling Relationship*, London: Darton, Longman and Todd.

Vanstone, W. H., 1982/1987, *The Stature of Waiting*, London: Darton, Longman and Todd.

Vanstone, W. H., 1979, *Love's Endeavour, Love's Expense*, London: Darton, Longman and Todd.

Chapter 2   Mind, Body and Spirit

Ellenberger, H., 1970, *The Discovery of the Unconscious: the History and Evolution of Dynamic Psychiatry*, New York: Basic Books.

Haule, John Ryan, 2011, *Jung in the 21st Century*, Vol. 1, London/New York: Routledge.

Jacobs, Michael, 2006, *The Presenting Past: The Core of Psychodynamic Counselling and Therapy*, 3rd edn, Maidenhead: Open University Press.

Jung, C. G., 1964/1978, *Man and his Symbols*, London: Pan Books.

Lear, Jonathan, 2005, *Freud*, New York and London: Routledge.

Skynner, R. and Cleese, J., 1983, *Families and How to Survive Them*, London: Methuen.

Wulff, D. H., 1997, *The Psychology of Religion*, New York: John Wiley and Sons.

Chapters 3 and 4   Nurture, Attachment and Love

Axline, Virginia, 1964, *Dibs: In Search of Self*, London: Pelican.

Bowlby, John, 1988/2005, *A Secure Base*, London: Routledge Classics.

Gerhardt, S., 2004, *Why Love Matters*, London: Routledge.

Solomon, A., 2012, *Far from the Tree*, NY: Simon & Schuster.

Winnicott, D. W., 1964, *The Child, the Family and the Outside World*, London: Penguin.

Winnicott, D. W.,1996, eds R. Shepherd, J. Johns, H. Taylor Robinson, *Thinking About Children*, London: Karnac Books.

Chapters 5 and 6   Sexuality

Cherin, Kim, 1999, *The Woman Who Gave Birth to Her Mother*, London: Penguin.

Cowan, Lyn, 1990, *Masochism – a Jungian View*, Dallas, TX: Spring Publications.

Guggenbuhl-Craig, A., 1971/1996, *Power in the Helping Professions*, trans. Myron Gubitz, Woodstock, CT: Spring Publications.

Imbens, A. and Jonker, I., 1992, *Christianity and Incest*, Tunbridge Wells: Burns and Oates.

Jukes, Adam, 1999, *Men who Batter Women*, London: Routledge.

Leonard, L. S., 1985, *The Wounded Woman: Healing the father-daughter relationship*, Boston and London: Shambhala.

Moore, R. and Gillette, D., 1991, *King, Warrior, Magician, Lover: Rediscovering the Archetypes of the Mature Masculine*, New York: HarperCollins.

Nelson, James, 1988, *The Intimate Connection: Male Sexuality, Male Spirituality*, Philadelphia: Westminster Press.

Paterson, M., 1997, *Singing for Our Lives: Positively Gay and Christian*, Sheffield: Cairns Publications.

Pinkola Estes, Clarissa, 2008, *Women Who Run with the Wolves*, London: Rider.

Quilliam, S., 2001, *Stop Arguing and Start Talking*, London: Relate Publications.

Rutter, Peter, 1989, *Sex in the Forbidden Zone*, New York: Ballantine Books.

Sanderson, Christiane, 2006, *Counselling Adult Survivors of Sexual Abuse*, London: Jessica Kingsley.

Teich, N. M., 2012, *Transgender 101: A Simple Guide to a Complex Issue*, New York: Columbia University Press.

Wilson, P. B., 2005, *Being Single in the Church*, London: Darton, Longman and Todd.

Chapters 7 and 8   Loss

Becker, E., 1975, *The Denial of Death*, New York: Free Press.

De Hennezel, M., 1997, *Intimate Death: how the Dying Teach Us to Live*, trans. Carol Brown Janeway, London: Warner Books.

Gregory of Nyssa, 1993, *On the Soul and Resurrection*, trans. C. P. Roth, Crestwood, NY: SVS Press.

Helen, Maggie, 2002, *Coping with Suicide*, London: Sheldon Press.

Jewett, C., 1984, *Helping Children Cope with Separation and Loss,* London: Batsford Press.

Lewis, C. S., 1961, *A Grief Observed*, London: Faber and Faber.

Raphael, B., 1984, *The Anatomy of Bereavement*, London: Unwin Hyman.

Stedeford, A., 1984, *Facing Death*, London: Heineman Medical Books.

Worden, J. W., 2009, *Grief Counselling and Grief Therapy*, 4th edn, London: Routledge.

Worden, J. W., 2002, *Children and Grief*, New York: Guildford Press.

Chapter 9   What is Mental Health?

Foskett, John, 1984, *Meaning in Madness: The Pastor and the Mentally Ill*, London: SPCK, New Library of Pastoral Care.

Laing, R. D., 1960, *The Divided Self*, London: Tavistock.

Storr, Anthony, 1989, *The Art of Psychotherapy*, London: Secker and Warburg/Heinemann.

Useful website: MIND: www.mind.org.uk

Chapter 10   Depression

Gale, Patrick, 2007, *Notes from an Exhibition* (novel), London: Harper.

Lewis, Gwyneth, 2002, *Sunbathing in the Rain: a Cheerful Book about Depression*, London: Harper Perennial.

Mursell, Gordon, 1989, *Out of the Deep: Prayer as Protest*, London: Darton, Longman and Todd.

Solomon, Andrew, 2002, *The Noonday Demon*, London: Vintage.

Styron, William, 1991, *Darkness Visible*, London: Jonathan Cape.

Waldron, Robert, 2012, *Acquainted with the Night: an Exploration of Spirituality and Depression*, London: Darton, Longman and Todd.

Useful website: Samaritans: www.samaritans.org

Chapter 11   Addiction

Doyle, R. and Nowinski, J., 2012, *Almost Alcoholic*, Center City, MN: Hazelden.

Flores, P. J., 2004, *Addiction as Attachment Disorder*, Maryland: Jason Aaronson.

Leech, Kenneth, 1998, *Drugs and Pastoral Care*, London: Darton, Longman and Todd.

Moss, A. C. and Dyer, K. R., 2010, *Psychology of Addictive Behaviour*, London: Palgrave Macmillan.

Ruscombe-King, Gillie and Hurst, Sheila, 1993, *Alcohol Problems: Talking with Drinkers*, London: Jessica Kingsley.

Webber, Meletios, 2003, *Steps of Transformation: an Orthodox Priest Explores the Twelve Steps*, New York: Conciliar Press.

Useful websites:

Alcoholics Anonymous: www.alcoholics-anonymous.org.uk/

Al-Anon: www.al-anonuk.org.uk/

Narcotics Anonymous: www.ukna.org/

Chapter 12   Eating Disorder

Bynum, C. W., 1987, *Holy Feast and Holy Fast*, Berkeley, CA: University of California Press.

Crilly, Lynn, 2012, *Hope with Eating Disorders: A self-help guide for parents, carers and friends of sufferers*, London: Hay House Publishing.

Fairburn, C. G., 2008, *Cognitive Behavior Therapy and Eating Disorders*, New York: Guilford Press.

Gordon, R. A., 2000, *Eating Disorder: Anatomy of a Social Epidemic*, Oxford: Blackwell.

Gross, Philip, 1998, *The Waiting Game* (poems), Newcastle: Bloodaxe Books.

Treasure, Janet, Smith, Grainne and Crane, Anna, 2007, Skills-based Learning for Caring for a Loved One with an Eating Disorder: The New Maudsley Method, London: Routledge.

Chapter 13   Schizophrenia and Other Psychotic Disorders

See also reading for Chapter 9

Compton, M. T. and Broussard, B., 2009, *The First Episode of Psychosis: A Guide for Patients and their Families*, New York: Oxford University Press.

Coyte, M.E., Gilbert, P., and Nicholls, V. (eds), 2007, *Spirituality, Values and Mental Health: Jewels for the Journey*, London: Jessica Kingsley.

Cox, Murray, 1987, *Mutative Metaphors in Psychotherapy*, London and New York: Tavistock.

Hemmings, Gwynneth, 1989, *Inside Schizophrenia*, London: Sidgwick and Jackson.

Useful websites:

MIND: www.mind.org.uk

Mental Health Advocacy: www.afmh.org.uk/

Chapter 14   Betrayal and Forgiveness

Bailie, Gil, 1995, *Violence Unveiled*, New York: Crossroad.

Moore, Sebastian, 1977, *The Crucified Jesus is No Stranger*, Mahwah, NJ: Paulist Press.

Olds, Sharon, 2012, *Stag's Leap* (poems), London: Jonathan Cape.

Shaffer, Peter, 1993, *The Gift of the Gorgon*, London: Penguin.

Williams, Rowan, 2000, *Christ on Trial: How the Gospel Unsettles our Judgement*, London: Fount.

Appendix   Reflecting on Your Pastoral Practice

Paterson, M. and Leach, Jane, 2010, *Pastoral Supervision: A Handbook*, London: SCM Press.

Whorton, Bob, 2011, *Reflective Caring*, London: SPCK.

Index of Authors Cited

Alison, James 74
Angelou, Maya 99

Basil the Great 37
Bowlby, John 39–41
Bruch, Hilda 191

Campbell, Alastair 3, 6
Chrysostom, John 5
Cleese, John 18
Cowan, Lyn 90

Dickens, Charles 120

Fiennes, William 156
Foskett, John 202–3
Fox, Kate 23
Freud, Sigmund 5–6, 16, 85,
    136, 152, 156
Fromm, Erich 90

Gale, Patrick 148–9
Gregory the Great 5
Gut, Emmy 153–4, 162

Hadjewich 56–7
Haule, John Ryan 17–18
Herbert, George 5
Holloway, Richard 78

Jukes, Adam 94–5
Jung, Carl Gustav 16, 169

Kafka, Franz 142
Klein, Melanie 112
Kristeva, Julia 156

Lewis, C. S. 90, 110, 112,
    115
Lewis, Gwyneth 153–4
Litchfield, Kate 98–9, 107,
    128 fn.
Lynch, Bernard 74

Malan, David 140
Maximus the Confessor 68,
    105
Merton, Thomas 6
Minuchin, Salvador 184
Moore, Sebastian 24–5,
    219

Nouwen, Henri 6

Park, Clare 183
Potok, Chaim 153

Rayner and Watson 20
Ridler, Anne 55
Rose, Jessica 76 fn.
Ross, Mabel 135
Rutter, Peter 82

Skynner, Robin 18
Solomon, Andrew 152, 156,

Stedeford, Averil 113
Stoller, Robert J. 84–6, 89
Styron, William 161–2

Vanstone, W. H. 7

Weatherhead, Leslie 5–6
Weil, Simone 89

Whorton, Bob 77
Winnicott, Donald 39–40, 41–3,
    52–3, 136,
Williams, H. A. 6

Yalom, I. D. 113

Index of Subjects and Biblical Names

abandonment 29, 48, 83, 84, 95, 150
Abraham 66, 106
absence 42–3, 51, 58, 87, 111
absolution 5, 207
abuse 175, 182, 186, 192, 210
  of drugs 146, 185
  sexual 98–103, 108, 151, 162, 211, 217, 230
acting out 49, 62, 85, 87–8, 140, 184
Adam 64, 74, 208, 221
addiction 34, 139, 164–78, 180, 186
adolescence 39, 40, 64, 87, 108, 120, 134, 182, 184, 185, 186, 193, 215
advocacy 201, 232
ageing 63, 107
aggression 42, 88, 89, 95, 122, 141
agoraphobia 114, 117
AIDS 158
amygdala 20–1
anger 24, 27, 29, 30, 38, 40, 42, 45, 57, 142, 150, 214
  and addiction 172, 175
  and depression 153, 155
  and eating disorder 184, 185, 188–9
  with God 160, 212
  in loss 111, 115, 116, 117, 118, 122, 124
  in masochism 86, 87, 89

and sectioning 201
and sexual abuse 100, 101
and suicide 149, 162–3
and violence 96
anointing 5
anorexia 179 – 83
  danger signals 191
  and family 184–7
  treatment 187
anxiety 6, 9, 19, 27, 34, 44, 45–6, 47–9, 52, 56, 59, 64, 93, 141
  and addiction 172
  and eating disorder 187, 191
  existential 148, 156
  and God 137, 207
  and grief 108, 110, 112, 113–14, 115, 117, 122, 123, 126, 128
  health 34
  and psychosis 198
  and sexuality 73, 185
  and suicide 162
  see also separation anxiety
archetype 16–17
Ascension 7, 106
asceticism 35
authority 7, 24, 25, 27, 35, 79, 82, 95, 142, 163, 189

baby 37–8, 41–3, 50–2, 106, 124, 151, 165, 208
baptism 9, 51–2
betrayal 36, 52, 91, 207–22

bipolar disorder 82, 145, 148–9, 158, 193, 198
bi-sexuality 73
blame 27, 54, 94–5, 100, 124, 187, 194
blankets 52
body 20, 33–5, 39, 62, 110, 112, 142, 147
    and abuse 100–2
    and addiction 168
    of Christ 37, 47, 68, 188
    death 105, 125
    eating disorder 179–84, 185, 187, 191–2
    of family 184
    gendered 67, 69–71
    of Jesus 91
bond 44, 50, 164
boundaries 50, 59, 67, 76, 83, 99, 100, 123, 167, 210
brain 17, 20, 25, 37–8
breakdown 41, 67, 220
    marital 89
breast 63, 106
bulimia 179, 183–4, 186–7
burn-out 21, 193, 210

celibacy 78
Child Protection Policy 99, 210
childhood 15, 21–2, 40–3, 86, 100, 102, 108, 141, 148, 149–50, 151, 162, 217, 220
Childline 100
Christ 3, 4, 6, 56–7, 58, 66, 81, 96, 98, 150, 211–12
    transcending gender 68
    see also body of Christ
clergy 4, 22, 25, 27, 74, 79, 83, 91, 127, 128
collective unconscious 16
collusion 57
Comforter 4, 106
communion 79, 81
community 4, 6–8, 9, 11, 16, 35–6,

37, 44, 47, 49, 52, 60, 61, 65, 76, 83, 96, 99, 103, 110, 122, 126–7, 136, 137, 138, 154, 168, 177, 190, 193, 196, 197, 198–200, 201, 207, 210, 212, 219, 223
compulsive care giving 44–5, 101
Confession 4–5, 78
confidence 45, 51, 52, 79, 215
confidentiality 98, 161
conflict 8, 16, 32, 139n, 147, 182, 186, 222
    inner 148, 152–3, 175
    unresolved 185
consciousness 11, 15–24, 54, 57, 87, 101, 209, 213, 219, 221
consistency 59, 140
cortex 17, 38
counselling 32, 96–7, 143, 152, 156, 157, 172
    bereavement 107, 128
    pastoral 6, 7
Creed 18, 115
crisis 7, 20, 124, 125, 144, 153, 175, 185, 198, 201
    of faith 115, 118, 130
Cross, the 5, 6, 106, 154
cross-dressing 70
crucifixion 58, 90

David 66, 209
defences 25–7, 159
delusions 139, 142–3, 194, 200, 202
denial 28, 101, 191, 213, 214, 218, 221, 222
    in addiction 168, 173, 175
    of another's reality 69
    in grief 119–121, 124
depressive tendency 141
deprivation 43, 168, 173, 190
desert 10, 15, 37, 159, 181
desire 10, 40, 43, 91, 141, 165, 181, 184, 220, 221, 222
    and addiction 165, 168

erotic 65, 70, 74, 83–4, 147
  for revenge 213
despair 9, 40, 82, 112, 115, 117,
  123, 152, 155, 158, 161
dis-ease 34, 36
dislike 20, 22, 30, 35
displacement 23, 29
distress 8, 42, 128, 137, 140, 150,
  188
divorce 45, 70
doubt 130, 212, 214
  self-doubt 100, 151
  See also crisis in faith
dreams 18, 19, 194
drugs 138, 147
  and addiction 171, 174, 176
  and depression 147, 148,
    156–7, 161
  and psychosis 143, 193–4,
    196–8, 201
  side effects 143, 157, 196

Easter 58, 91, 149–50, 154
ECT 157
ego see 'I'
emotion 19–20, 139–40, 152
empathy 138
envy 29, 31, 77
ethics 72
Eucharist 5, 57, 76
existential anxiety 75, 148, 156
Eve 64, 66, 208

failure 102, 176, 212
  maternal 42
  in dependency 95
  of care 210
faith 6, 8, 10–11, 35, 55, 56, 63,
  82, 83, 158, 160
  questioning 115–8
  see also crisis of faith
Fall, the 66, 95, 208, 221
fantasy 142
  sexual 85–8

fasting 35, 180, 191
Father, the 3, 4, 58, 105
father 63, 64, 67, 82–3, 87, 109,
  114, 120, 122, 144, 151, 154,
  172, 185, 187, 195, 209–10,
  211
  applied to clergy 103
  spiritual 15
fear 20, 24, 30, 38, 56–7, 100,
  110, 113, 114, 115, 141, 171,
  175, 195, 201
  of abandonment 84
  of betrayal 52
  of breakdown 41
  of death 117
  of dependency 52
  of intimacy 141, 175
  irrational 19
  of persecution 93
  sexual 101
fetish 53
fight-flight 21
forgiveness 98, 207–22
friendship 33, 50, 65, 98, 162, 210
funeral 8, 71, 110–11, 121, 126,
  127, 130
  planning funeral visit 124

gender identity 62, 64, 95
genes 17
guilt 6, 21, 24, 27, 42, 54–5, 146,
  151, 172–3, 192, 199, 207, 209
  and abuse 100, 111
  and grief 112, 114–15, 117
  irrational 148, 155
  and masochism 85–91
  and suicide 123, 149, 163

Hamlet 109, 195
hate 94
healing 103, 112, 168
  Christ's 81, 90
  God's 217
  intercession for 6, 207

and transference 24
relationship 50–2, 167
sexuality 65, 67, 77, 81–4
space 117
techniques 138
hell 57, 155
heterosexual orientation 73, 74
homosexual orientation 72–3
hope 8, 104, 116, 126, 149, 150,
    154, 169
hospital 8, 19, 40, 43, 53, 125,
    153, 181–2, 186, 224
and addiction 177
admissions 42, 148, 161
and schizophrenia 197–202 see
    also sectioning
hostility 85, 88, 141, 209
human nature 62
hypocrisy 74, 79
hysterical tendency 139–40

'I', the 25, 30–1
ideas of reference 194
illusion 36, 65
insight 11, 35, 36, 203
lack of 139, 142–3
incarnation 7, 104
interdependence 33, 47, 137
intimacy 51, 66, 106, 140, 150,
    190
fear of 141–2
physical 76
risks of 81, 83
sexual 86
introjection 19, 27, 214
Isaac 97

Jacob 66, 67
jealousy 43
Jeremiah 104
Jesus 6, 7, 58, 63, 66, 68, 91,
    105–6, 154, 194, 202
John (Apostle) 58, 154
Joseph 66, 104

Judith 66
Judas 91

Lent 149
Lev, Asher 153–4
Little Albert 20

loneliness 69, 78, 80, 112, 127, 164
and solitude 75
love 16, 33, 36, 37, 56–8, 67, 84,
    88, 90, 94, 97, 98, 108, 116,
    123, 152–3, 214–5
and attachment 39–46, 52
of Christ 3, 91, 98
erotic 64–6, 209
falling in 18, 24
of God 4, 7, 8, 47, 56, 58
romantic 63
sexualisation of 101
tough 173
of the Trinity 58
marriage 5, 8, 10, 61, 62, 65, 75,
    77, 78, 96–7, 111, 153, 208,
    210, 212
masochism 81, 85–91, 92
memory 15, 19–22, 87, 147, 161–2
loss 158
recovered 99, 101–2
mental map 18, 19, 25
MIND 201
mind 15–20, 33–5, 53, 62, 67, 85,
    100, 110, 119, 137, 147, 152,
    169, 179, 196
mood 15, 88, 145–6, 180
swings 148, 155, 157, 193, 194
mother 53–4, 63, 64, 67, 102, 120,
    129, 151, 154, 175, 208
'good-enough' 41–3
spiritual 15
virgin 66

obesity 179, 184
obsessive-compulsive tendency
    139, 141, 142

omnipotence 39
One, the 56
Ophelia 195
orientation See heterosexual,
    homosexual
'Over-I' 27

paedophile 98
panic 19, 20, 43, 101, 102, 147
Paradise 104
paranoia 30, 112, 114–15, 213,
    215–16, 222
participation 3, 8, 36
Passion (of Christ) 188
passions 10, 66
perversion 84–5
Peter (Apostle) 3, 91, 212
pets, death of 108
post-natal depression 50–2, 151
power 15, 16, 36, 44, 47, 69, 95,
    116, 187
    abuse of 92
    creative 62
    food as 188–9
    healing 90
    in pastoral relationships 81–3,
        91
prayer 5, 8, 15, 18, 33, 37, 51, 59,
    83, 101, 117, 207, 223, 225,
    227
    for the dead 129
    Lord's Prayer 217
    and psalms 147
    Serenity Prayer 171
pre-menstrual dysphoric disorder
    (PMDD) 150
prison 8, 26, 73, 197–8
projection 29–33, 35
Psalms 53, 111, 146–7, 158, 159
psychoanalysis 5, 41
psychologizing 35
psychosis 138–9, 142–3, 193–200
psychotherapy 5, 22, 138, 143,
    156–8, 161, 197

Rachel 66, 104
rage 29, 43, 95, 188–9, 192, 220,
    222
rape 99, 220
reaction formation 28–9
Rebecca 66
reflection 8, 18, 21, 32, 56, 58, 61
regression 48
rejection 52, 75, 118, 140, 155,
    162
repentance 4
repressed memory 19–20, 101
responsibility 35, 48, 56, 59, 64,
    88, 90, 95, 170, 177, 212, 218,
    226
    pastoral 4, 175

resurrection 3, 7, 90–1, 105–6,
    115, 150, 159
risk 48, 55, 57, 75, 136, 171, 181,
    185, 211, 216, 222
    suicide 123–4, 157, 160
ritual 8, 11, 52, 83, 91, 216
    in grief 110–11, 117, 122
    obsessive 142
    sexual 85
role
    deviant 136
    fantasy 142
    gender 69
    models 66
    pastoral 6, 47, 50, 52, 82, 109,
        191, 227

sacrament 11, 216
sadism 81, 85–8, 92
Samaritans 160
Saul 209
schizoid tendency 139, 141–2
school 19, 21, 22, 49, 67, 73–4,
    107, 111, 120–1, 151–2
scripts 15–16
sectioning 200–2
security 6, 41, 101, 170

self 27–8, 30–3, 34, 41, 43, 62, 74,
    98, 100, 112, 116, 117, 158,
    173, 182, 201
    awareness 36, 56, 139
    betrayal 213, 214–15, 221
    care 21
    control 181
    deception 82
    discipline 183
    disgust 189, 215
    doubt 151
    esteem 141, 152, 186
    false 186
    harm 88, 128
    hatred 24, 146, 192
    image 96, 184, 187
    knowledge 33
    reflection 8
    reliance 39, 44–5, 48, 51, 52,
        57, 173, 209
    reproach 152, 162
    understanding 36, 67, 81
separation 10, 34, 69, 122, 162
    anxiety 43, 45, 53–4, 95
sexual abuse see abuse, sexual
shame 64, 72, 78, 86, 100, 162,
    174, 175, 184
siblings 19, 42, 64, 182, 186, 190
solitude 37, 75
somatization 34
soul 146, 159, 165, 209
Spirit 4, 11
spirit 33–4, 55, 62, 147, 170, 179,
    184, 192, 220
spiritualizing 35
stress 54, 130, 139, 193, 194
    and addiction 164, 172
    and depression 154, 155, 162
    and eating disorder 181–3, 184,
        188
suffering 90, 97, 154, 217
suicide 82, 123–4, 140, 148, 153,
    157, 160–3, 183, 185, 200

superego . See 'Over-I'
support 212
    in addiction 176–7
    in depression 163
    for pastor 227
    in grief 104, 109, 114, 118,
        121, 122, 124, 126, 127
    in psychosis 143
survival 17, 20, 25–8, 36, 37, 43,
    53, 59, 88, 113, 155, 172, 214,
    223
symbol 65, 84
    food as 188

Tamar 66
teddy bears 52
tenderness 64, 65, 66
therapist 24, 113, 176, 184
therapy 18, 73, 148, 176
    cognitive behavioural 187, 197
    drug 150
    electro-convulsive (ECT)
        157–8
    family 197
    group 197
transference 22–5, 35
transgendered 69–72
transitional object 52–3, 59
transsexual 22–5
trust 54–9, 79, 100, 105, 174,
    208–11, 213, 221

unconscious, the 19–27, 30–3, 35,
    56, 77, 101, 169

victim 85, 89, 92, 95, 103
    mind-set 97–8
vocation 75, 214, 215

wounds 83, 90, 130, 146
    of the Passion 58
widow 4
worship 4, 7, 8, 90